First Edition: 2024

Publication Year: 2024

i

What Makes The

MARKETING CAMPAIGN

Successful

By

AKSHAT SINGH BISHT

INTRODUCTION

Welcome to the world of marketing excellence encapsulated within the pages of **What Makes The Marketing Campaign Successful** Here, we embark on a journey through the captivating realm of iconic marketing campaigns that have not only shaped industries but also captured the hearts and minds of consumers worldwide.

Within these chapters lie the narratives of brands that dared to challenge the ordinary, to redefine norms, and to etch themselves into the annals of marketing history. From the whimsical antics of Snickers' "You're Not You When You're Hungry" to the empowering ethos of Nike's "Just Do It," each campaign serves as a beacon of innovation and ingenuity in a crowded marketplace.

At the heart of this exploration lies a deep commitment to unraveling the mysteries of marketing mastery. We delve into the intricacies of campaign development, from the initial spark of inspiration to the meticulous execution that drives consumer engagement. Through a lens of research, strategy, and creativity, we dissect the anatomy of success, uncovering the methodologies that underpin enduring brand resonance.

Yet, beyond the mechanics of marketing, lies a profound appreciation for the art of storytelling. Within these campaigns, we discover narratives that transcend mere product promotion, weaving tales that resonate with the human experience. From moments of humor to instances of profound insight, each campaign serves as a testament to the enduring power of authentic connection.

As you turn the pages of **What Makes The Marketing Campaign Successful**, prepare to be inspired, educated, and entertained by the stories that have shaped modern marketing. Whether you are a seasoned industry professional or an aspiring marketer, this book offers a treasure trove of insights and wisdom to inform your own endeavors.

Join us as we embark on a voyage of discovery, unraveling the secrets behind some of the most iconic campaigns in history. Together, let us celebrate the art and science of marketing excellence, one chapter at a time.

Welcome To
What Makes The Marketing Campaign Successful.

MORE ABOUT BOOK

In the ever-evolving world of marketing, certain campaigns stand out as iconic landmarks, shaping consumer culture and leaving a lasting imprint on the collective consciousness. "What Makes The Marketing Campaign Successful" delves into the captivating narratives behind these landmark campaigns, offering insights into the creative genius, strategic vision, and cultural resonance that propelled them to legendary status. From the humorous antics of Snickers' "You're Not You When You're Hungry" to the empowering ethos of Nike's "Just Do It," each chapter of this book explores the genesis, execution, and enduring impact of these iconic marketing endeavors. Through meticulous research, insightful analysis, and compelling storytelling, we uncover the secrets behind their success and glean invaluable lessons for marketers, entrepreneurs, and enthusiasts alike.

The story of Snickers' iconic campaign begins with a simple yet profound insight: hunger affects more than just the stomach. Through extensive market research, Snickers unearthed the universal truth that hunger can alter mood, behavior, and perception, leaving individuals feeling "not themselves." Armed with this insight, Snickers crafted a campaign that tapped into the shared human experience of hunger, using humor and empathy to create a connection with consumers. From memorable television commercials to interactive social media campaigns, Snickers' "You're Not You When You're Hungry" campaign became a cultural phenomenon, driving brand awareness and sales while leaving a lasting impression on audiences worldwide. This chapter explores the strategic thinking, creative execution, and enduring legacy of one of the most successful marketing campaigns of modern times.

Nike's "Just Do It" campaign is not just a slogan; it's a rallying cry for athletes and dreamers alike. Born out of the desire to inspire and empower, "Just Do It" encapsulates Nike's ethos of relentless pursuit and unwavering determination. Through powerful storytelling and iconic imagery, Nike transformed a simple phrase into a global movement, transcending sports and resonating with individuals across cultures and generations. This chapter delves into the origins of the "Just Do It" campaign, exploring the strategic decisions, creative executions, and cultural impact that propelled Nike to the forefront of athletic apparel and footwear. From groundbreaking advertisements to high-profile endorsements, Nike's "Just Do It" campaign exemplifies the power of brand storytelling and the enduring appeal of a compelling message.

Dove's "Real Beauty" campaign challenged conventional beauty standards and celebrated the diversity and authenticity of women's bodies. Rooted in the belief that beauty comes in all shapes, sizes, and colors, Dove sought to redefine the conversation around beauty and empower women to embrace their unique features. Through thought-provoking advertisements, social media campaigns, and grassroots initiatives, Dove sparked a global conversation about self-esteem, body image, and the impact of media representation on women's perceptions of beauty. This chapter examines the strategic objectives, creative executions, and societal impact of Dove's "Real Beauty" campaign, highlighting the brand's commitment to authenticity, inclusivity, and social responsibility.

Old Spice's "The Man Your Man Could Smell Like" campaign revolutionized the way men's grooming products were marketed, injecting humor, wit, and irreverence into a traditionally conservative industry. Through a series of viral advertisements featuring the charismatic "Old Spice Guy," the brand redefined masculinity and appealed to a new generation of consumers. This chapter explores the strategic thinking, creative executions, and cultural impact of Old Spice's campaign, highlighting the brand's ability to reinvent itself and stay relevant in an ever-changing marketplace.

M&M's "Become a Character" campaign transformed colorful chocolate candies into beloved characters with distinct personalities and quirks. Through a series of whimsical advertisements and interactive online experiences, M&M's engaged consumers in a playful and immersive brand experience, driving brand affinity and loyalty. This chapter delves into the creative process, strategic objectives, and consumer engagement tactics employed by M&M's to bring its iconic characters to life, highlighting the brand's ability to connect with audiences on an emotional level.

L'Oreal's "Because You're Worth It" campaign redefined beauty advertising by shifting the focus from product features to consumer empowerment. By emphasizing self-worth, confidence, and individuality, L'Oreal challenged traditional beauty norms and inspired women to embrace their unique beauty. This chapter explores the strategic evolution of L'Oreal's campaign, from its inception in the 1970s to its continued relevance in the digital age, highlighting the brand's commitment to diversity, inclusivity, and empowerment.

Maybelline's "Maybe She's Born With It, Maybe It's Maybelline" campaign celebrated the transformative power of makeup and the confidence it can inspire in women. Through aspirational advertisements featuring glamorous models and catchy slogans, Maybelline positioned itself as a beauty authority and a champion of self-expression. This chapter examines the strategic objectives, creative executions, and cultural impact of Maybelline's campaign, highlighting the brand's ability to resonate with consumers and stay relevant in a competitive market.

"What Makes The Marketing Campaign Successful" is more than just a collection of case studies; it's a testament to the power of creativity, storytelling, and strategic thinking in the world of marketing. From Snickers' humorous take on hunger to Nike's empowering ethos of determination, each campaign exemplifies the transformative potential of advertising to shape perceptions, influence behaviors, and inspire change. As we reflect on the stories behind these iconic campaigns, we are reminded of the enduring lessons they hold for marketers, entrepreneurs, and storytellers alike. Whether it's the importance of authenticity, the value of empathy, or the impact of a compelling message, these campaigns offer invaluable insights into the art and science of marketing excellence. As we look to the future, let us draw inspiration from these iconic campaigns and continue to push the boundaries of creativity, innovation, and impact in the ever-evolving landscape of marketing.

CONTENTS

1

A BITE OUT OF HUNGER HOW SNICKERS' "YOU'RE NOT YOU WHEN YOU'RE HUNGRY" BECAME A MARKETING ICON

Snickers, a brand under Mars, Incorporated, is one of the world's most beloved chocolate bars. Over the years, Snickers has become synonymous with satisfaction and energy, thanks to its catchy slogan "You're Not You When You're Hungry." This case study delves into the success of Snickers' iconic campaign, exploring its inception, execution, impact, and lasting legacy.

The "You're Not You When You're Hungry" campaign is a marketing initiative by Snickers, a popular chocolate bar brand owned by Mars, Incorporated. This campaign has been widely successful and memorable, employing humorous scenarios where people exhibit out of character behavior due to hunger, only to return to normal after eating a Snickers bar.

The commercials typically feature someone acting irritable, irrational, or just not themselves because they are hungry. Then, after consuming a Snickers bar, they revert to their usual selves, accompanied by the tagline "You're Not You When You're Hungry."

This campaign has been running for several years and has included various celebrities and fictional characters, such as Betty White, Joe Pesci, and the characters from the television series "The Brady Bunch," among others. It's known for its humorous and relatable approach to highlighting the satisfying nature of Snickers bars.

Snickers, a renowned chocolate brand under the umbrella of Mars, Incorporated, has a rich history dating back to its introduction in 1930. Named after the favorite horse of the Mars family, Snickers quickly gained popularity for its distinctive combination of nougat, caramel, peanuts, and milk chocolate, becoming one of the best selling candy bars worldwide. Before the launch of the "You're Not You When You're Hungry" campaign, Snickers had established itself as a popular chocolate bar with a focus on satisfying hunger. However, Mars, Incorporated recognized the need to refresh the brand's image and engage consumers in a more memorable and relatable way.

The "You're Not You When You're Hungry" campaign was conceptualized by the advertising agency BBDO in 2010. The central idea behind the campaign was to humorously illustrate how hunger can alter a person's behavior and personality, ultimately emphasizing the need for a satisfying Snickers bar to return to one's normal self.

Over the years, Snickers has maintained its status as a beloved treat, but by the late 2000s, the brand faced a challenge. Despite its strong legacy and recognition, Snickers encountered stagnating sales and struggled to maintain relevance in an increasingly competitive confectionery market.

Consumer preferences were evolving, with health conscious trends influencing snack choices, posing a threat to traditional candy bars like Snickers. Moreover, amidst a plethora of snack options, Snickers needed to find a way to differentiate itself and rekindle consumer interest.

Recognizing the need for innovation and rejuvenation, Snickers embarked on a journey to revitalize its brand image and reignite consumer excitement. This imperative led to the inception of the iconic "You're Not You When You're Hungry" campaign, which would prove to be a turning point in Snickers' marketing strategy.

The campaign's genesis lay in profound insights derived from extensive market research. Snickers identified a universal truth: hunger affects not only physical wellbeing but also mood and behavior. Leveraging this understanding, Snickers sought to position itself not merely as a chocolate bar but as a solution to the common problem of hunger induced irritability and decreased performance.

Thus, against the backdrop of evolving consumer preferences and a need for reinvention, Snickers embarked on a journey to transform its brand perception and reclaim its position as a beloved snack choice. The "You're Not You When You're Hungry" campaign would emerge as a testament to Snickers' ability to adapt, innovate, and connect with consumers on a deeper, more emotional level.

Why the campaign was launched:

The "You're Not You When You're Hungry" campaign was launched in response to several key challenges that Snickers faced, below are the few key challenges:

1. Declining Relevance and Sales:

Snickers, despite being a well established brand with a loyal consumer base, experienced stagnating sales and diminishing relevance in the highly competitive confectionery market. Emerging health conscious trends and a plethora of snack options posed a threat to traditional candy bars like Snickers. The brand needed to find a way to differentiate itself and capture the attention of evolving consumer preferences.

2. Perception as Just Another Chocolate Bar:

Over time, Snickers risked being perceived as just another chocolate bar among consumers. Despite its iconic status and distinctive flavor profile, the brand struggled to stand out amidst a sea of snack choices. There was a need to redefine Snickers' brand identity and communicate its unique value proposition to consumers effectively.

3. Understanding Consumer Behavior:

Through extensive market research, Snickers identified a crucial insight: hunger not only affects physical wellbeing but also influences mood and behavior. Leveraging this understanding, Snickers aimed to position itself as more than just a satisfying snack; it sought to become a solution to the problem of hunger induced irritability and decreased performance.

4. Rejuvenating Brand Image:

Snickers recognized the importance of innovation and reinvention to stay relevant in a dynamic market landscape. The brand needed to revitalize its image, reconnect with consumers, and reignite excitement around its products. The "You're Not You When You're Hungry" campaign presented an opportunity to transform Snickers' brand perception and deepen emotional connections with consumers.

In essence, the campaign was launched to address these challenges by leveraging humor, relatability, and a profound understanding of consumer behavior to reposition Snickers as more than just a chocolate bar – it was positioned as a solution to hunger induced mood swings, offering consumers a way to return to their best selves.

What were the campaign objectives:

The campaign objectives for Snickers' "You're Not You When You're Hungry" campaign were designed to align with the brand's overall marketing and business goals. These objectives provided a roadmap for the campaign's strategy and execution, guiding efforts to maximize effectiveness and drive measurable results. The objectives included:

1. Increase Brand Awareness:

One of the primary objectives of the campaign was to raise awareness of the Snickers brand and its association with satisfying hunger. By leveraging memorable and relatable messaging,

Snickers aimed to enhance brand recall and visibility among its target audience, ultimately solidifying its position as a top of mind snack choice.

2. Drive Engagement and Interaction:

Snickers sought to engage consumers in meaningful interactions with the brand, both online and offline. Through creative storytelling and social media engagement, the campaign aimed to spark conversations, encourage user generated content, and foster a sense of community around the brand. By driving engagement, Snickers aimed to deepen consumer connections and build brand loyalty over time.

3. Communicate Product Benefits:

The campaign aimed to effectively communicate the benefits of Snickers bars as a satisfying and energizing snack option. By highlighting the product's ability to curb hunger and restore energy levels, Snickers aimed to reinforce its value proposition and differentiate itself from competitors. The campaign sought to position Snickers as the go to solution for hunger induced mood swings and cravings.

4. Generate Sales and Revenue:

Ultimately, the campaign aimed to drive tangible business results by increasing sales and revenue for Snickers bars. By leveraging compelling messaging and strategic marketing initiatives, Snickers aimed to stimulate consumer demand and drive purchase intent. The campaign's success would be measured by its impact on sales volume, market share, and overall business performance.

5. Create Emotional Connection:

Snickers aimed to create an emotional connection with consumers by tapping into universal experiences and emotions related to hunger and satisfaction. Through humor, empathy, and authenticity, the campaign sought to resonate with consumers on a deeper level, forging strong emotional bonds with the brand. By fostering emotional connection, Snickers aimed to build long term brand affinity and loyalty among consumers.

6. Win Awards and Recognition:

While not the primary objective, Snickers aimed to achieve recognition and acclaim within the advertising industry through the campaign. By delivering creative excellence and innovative storytelling, Snickers aimed to earn awards, accolades, and positive press coverage. The campaign's success in winning industry awards would serve as external validation of its effectiveness and creativity.

Overall, these campaign objectives guided Snickers' strategic approach and informed its decision making throughout the "You're Not You When You're Hungry" campaign, ensuring alignment with broader marketing goals and driving measurable impact on brand awareness, engagement, sales, and emotional connection with consumers.

The Big Idea: You vs. You When You're Hungry

The campaign's core idea is simple: hunger transforms people into exaggerated versions of themselves. Snickers positions itself as the solution, restoring normalcy with a satisfying bite.

The strategy behind the campaign:

Well we have covered the introduction, objectives and problems that snickers faced. Let's dive deep into the marketing strategy.

1. Identifying the Target Audience: Snickers' marketing strategy for the "You're Not You When You're Hungry" campaign began with a clear understanding of their target audience. They aimed to reach consumers of all ages who could relate to the feeling of hunger induced mood swings and cravings for a satisfying snack. By targeting a broad demographic, Snickers ensured that their message would resonate with a wide range of consumers.

2. Leveraging Humor and Relatability: The cornerstone of Snickers' marketing strategy was the use of humor and relatability to capture the attention of consumers. The campaign's advertisements depicted exaggerated scenarios of people behaving out of character due to hunger, creating a sense of amusement and recognition among viewers. By tapping into the universal experience of feeling "hangry," Snickers effectively connected with audiences on an emotional level, making their brand message memorable and engaging.

3. Emphasizing the Product Benefit: Central to Snickers' marketing strategy was the emphasis on the product's benefit – satisfying hunger and returning consumers to their normal selves. The campaign highlighted Snickers bars as the solution to hunger induced mood swings, positioning them as a go to snack for satisfying cravings and restoring energy levels. By showcasing the product in action within the context of relatable scenarios, Snickers reinforced its value proposition and differentiated itself from competitors.

4. Creating a Memorable Tagline: The campaign's tagline, "You're Not You When You're Hungry," played a crucial role in Snickers' marketing strategy. This simple yet impactful phrase served as a unifying theme across all advertisements, reinforcing the brand message and creating consistency in communication. The tagline quickly became synonymous with Snickers, making it instantly recognizable to consumers and reinforcing brand recall.

5. Multi Channel Marketing Approach: Snickers employed a Multi Channel marketing approach to maximize the campaign's reach and impact. In addition to traditional television commercials and print advertisements, Snickers leveraged digital platforms and social media to engage with consumers online. By creating shareable content and encouraging user participation through hashtags like #EatASNICKERS, Snickers extended the campaign's reach beyond traditional media channels, fostering greater brand awareness and interaction.

6. Integration with Pop Culture and Events: Another key aspect of Snickers' marketing strategy was the integration of the campaign with pop culture and events. The brand collaborated with celebrities, sports personalities, and influencers to further amplify its message and reach new audiences. Additionally, Snickers capitalized on cultural moments and events to create timely and relevant content that resonated with consumers. By staying current and culturally relevant, Snickers ensured that its campaign remained top of mind and engaging to consumers.

7. Measuring and Optimizing Performance: Throughout the campaign, Snickers continuously measured and evaluated the performance of its marketing efforts. By tracking key metrics such as brand awareness, engagement, and sales, Snickers gained valuable insights into the effectiveness of its strategy and made adjustments as needed to optimize performance. This data driven approach allowed Snickers to refine its messaging, target audience, and channels to maximize ROI and achieve its marketing objectives.

Snickers' marketing strategy for the "You're Not You When You're Hungry" campaign was characterized by a focus on humor, relatability, and product benefits. By leveraging these elements across multiple channels and integrating with pop culture, Snickers successfully connected with consumers, driving brand awareness, engagement, and sales. Through careful measurement and optimization, Snickers ensured that its campaign remained effective and impactful, leaving a lasting impression on consumers worldwide.

The marketing research conducted for Snickers' "You're Not You When You're Hungry" campaign was exhaustive and illuminating. Through a combination of qualitative and quantitative methods, researchers delved deep into the psychology of hunger, seeking to understand its profound effects on consumers' emotions, behaviors, and decision-making process, below are the few highlights of the marketing research.

1. Consumer Insights: Snickers conducted extensive market research to gain insights into consumer behavior, attitudes, and preferences related to snacking and hunger. This research included surveys, focus groups, and in depth interviews to understand how hunger impacts people's mood and decision making processes. Through this research, Snickers identified the universal experience of feeling "hangry" as a key insight that could be leveraged in their marketing campaign.

2. Competitive Analysis: In addition to understanding consumer behavior, Snickers also conducted a thorough competitive analysis to assess the landscape of the confectionery industry. This analysis included studying competitor products, marketing strategies, and messaging to identify opportunities for differentiation and positioning. By understanding the strengths and weaknesses of competitors, Snickers was able to carve out a unique space for itself with the "You're Not You When You're Hungry" campaign.

3. Target Audience Segmentation: Snickers segmented its target audience based on demographic, psychographic, and behavioral factors to tailor its marketing efforts effectively. This segmentation allowed Snickers to identify specific consumer groups who were most likely to resonate with the campaign's message and creative execution. By understanding the unique needs and preferences of each segment, Snickers was able to develop targeted marketing strategies that spoke directly to their interests and motivations.

4. Concept Testing: Before launching the campaign, Snickers conducted concept testing to gauge consumer reactions to different creative concepts and messaging. This involved presenting potential campaign ideas to focus groups or through online surveys to gather feedback on overall appeal, clarity, and effectiveness. By testing multiple concepts, Snickers was able to refine its approach and ensure that the final campaign resonated with its target audience.

5. Media Planning and Optimization: Snickers conducted media research to identify the most effective channels and placements for reaching its target audience. This involved analyzing media consumption habits, audience demographics, and advertising trends to inform decisions around television, print, digital, and social media advertising. By optimizing media plans based on research insights, Snickers maximized the impact and efficiency of its marketing budget.

6. Measurement and Evaluation: Throughout the campaign, Snickers continuously monitored and evaluated key performance metrics to assess the effectiveness of its marketing efforts. This included tracking brand awareness, ad recall, consumer engagement, and sales impact to gauge the campaign's success. By measuring performance against predefined objectives, Snickers was able to identify areas of strength and opportunities for improvement, informing future marketing initiatives.

7. Post Campaign Analysis: After the campaign concluded, Snickers conducted a comprehensive Post Campaign analysis to assess overall effectiveness and ROI. This involved analyzing sales data, consumer feedback, and brand sentiment to evaluate the campaign's impact on brand perception and market share. By identifying successes and learnings from the campaign, Snickers was able to refine its marketing strategies for future initiatives and maintain its competitive edge in the marketplace.

The Insight: Hangry is Real

Research revealed a relatable truth: hunger makes people irritable, grumpy, and prone to outbursts. Snickers tapped into this concept, coining the now famous term "hangry" (hungry + angry).

Marketing research played a critical role in informing Snickers' "You're Not You When You're Hungry" campaign, providing insights into consumer behavior, competitive dynamics, target audience segmentation, creative concept testing, media planning, and performance measurement. By leveraging research insights throughout the campaign lifecycle, Snickers was able to develop a compelling marketing strategy that resonated with consumers and drove business results.

Buyer Persona for the campaign:

When we talk about campaigns and insights it is necessary to know who is your target market and customer. Let's describe the buyer persona for the campaign.

Name: Hungry Hannah

Background: Hannah is a 28 year old professional working in a fast paced corporate environment. She often finds herself juggling multiple deadlines and responsibilities, leading to long hours at the office and irregular meal times. Despite her busy schedule, Hannah prioritizes her health and tries to maintain a balanced diet, but she occasionally succumbs to unhealthy snacking habits when hunger strikes.

Demographics:

- Age: 28
- Gender: Female
- Occupation: Corporate professional
- Education: Bachelor's degree
- Income: Middle to upper middle class
- Location: Urban area

Psychographics:

- Personality: Hardworking, ambitious, and conscientious
- Values: Health and wellbeing, convenience, and efficiency
- Lifestyle: Active and on the go, often working late hours
- Interests: Fitness, cooking, and socializing with friends

Challenges:

1. **Hunger Pangs:** Hannah frequently experiences hunger pangs due to her busy schedule and irregular meal times, leading to decreased energy levels and mood swings.
2. **Time Constraints:** Hannah struggles to find time for proper meals amidst her demanding work schedule, often resorting to quick and convenient snacks to curb her hunger.
3. **Cravings:** When hunger strikes, Hannah tends to crave indulgent and satisfying snacks that provide instant gratification and energy boost.

Goals:

1. Satisfying Hunger: Hannah seeks convenient and satisfying snack options that can help her stay energized and focused throughout the day.
2. **Healthy Choices:** Despite occasional indulgences, Hannah aims to make healthier snacking choices that align with her overall wellness goals.
3. **Time Management:** Hannah wants snack options that fit seamlessly into her busy lifestyle and can be enjoyed on the go without sacrificing taste or quality.

How Snickers Meets Hannah's Needs:

Satisfying Hunger: Snickers' "You're Not You When You're Hungry" campaign resonates with Hannah's experience of feeling irritable and unfocused when hungry. The campaign's message reinforces Snickers bars as a satisfying and indulgent snack choice that can quickly curb hunger and restore energy levels, allowing Hannah to regain her focus and productivity.

Healthy Balance: While Snickers is known for its indulgent chocolate and caramel goodness, the campaign emphasizes the importance of satisfying hunger with a satisfying snack, aligning with Hannah's desire to make balanced snacking choices. The campaign's humor and relatability help Hannah feel less guilty about indulging in a Snickers bar occasionally while maintaining her overall wellness goals.

Convenience: Snickers bars are readily available at convenience stores, vending machines, and grocery stores, making them a convenient snack option for Hannah's busy lifestyle. The campaign's emphasis on the tagline "You're Not You When You're Hungry" serves as a reminder for Hannah to keep a Snickers bar handy for those moments when hunger strikes unexpectedly.

Key Takeaways: Hannah represents a key buyer persona for Snickers' "You're Not You When You're Hungry" campaign, embodying the challenges, goals, and preferences of busy professionals seeking convenient and satisfying snack options. By understanding Hannah's needs and motivations, Snickers can tailor its marketing messages and product offerings to effectively resonate with similar consumers, driving engagement and sales.

The marketing funnel, also known as the purchase funnel or sales funnel, represents the consumer journey from awareness to purchase. Analyzing how Snickers' campaign navigated this funnel provides insights into its effectiveness in driving brand awareness, engagement, and ultimately, sales. Lets discuss the marketing funnel is respect to the campaign.

Awareness Stage:

Objective: The primary goal at this stage was to generate awareness of the campaign and its central message: "You're Not You When You're Hungry."

Strategy: Snickers utilized a mix of traditional and digital channels, including television commercials, print ads, and social media platforms, to reach a broad audience. The humorous and attention grabbing nature of the ads helped in capturing viewers' attention and driving initial brand awareness.

Metrics: Key metrics at this stage included reach, impressions, and brand recall. Snickers aimed to ensure that the campaign message resonated with consumers and left a lasting impression.

Interest and Consideration Stage:

Objective: After capturing consumers' attention, the next step was to foster interest and consideration for the Snickers brand and its products.

Strategy: Snickers focused on creating engaging content that encouraged further interaction with the brand. This included interactive digital experiences, behind the scenes footage, and user generated content campaigns where consumers shared their own "You're Not You When You're Hungry" moments.

Metrics: Metrics such as website traffic, social media engagement (likes, shares, comments), and video views were important indicators of consumer interest and engagement with the campaign content.

Desire Stage:

Objective: Once consumers were aware of the campaign and interested in the brand, the goal was to stimulate desire and preference for Snickers over competing products.

Strategy: Snickers leveraged persuasive messaging and emotional storytelling to deepen consumers' connection with the brand. Ads emphasized the transformative power of Snickers in alleviating hunger induced mood swings and returning individuals to their best selves.

Metrics: Brand sentiment, purchase intent, and consideration metrics were used to gauge consumers' inclination towards Snickers and their likelihood to choose it over alternative snack options.

Action Stage:

Objective: The final stage of the funnel involved converting consumer interest and desire into action, i.e., purchasing Snickers products.

Strategy: Snickers employed various tactics to facilitate the purchase process, including promotional offers, in store displays, and online purchase incentives. The campaign's memorable tagline and imagery reinforced the association between hunger, mood swings, and the need for Snickers, prompting consumers to make a purchase.

Metrics: Sales data, conversion rates, and market share growth were key metrics used to measure the campaign's success in driving tangible business outcomes.

Retention and Advocacy:

Objective: Beyond the initial purchase, Snickers aimed to foster long term customer loyalty and advocacy.

Strategy: The brand continued to engage with consumers through post purchase communications, loyalty programs, and ongoing content creation. By maintaining a consistent brand presence and delivering on its promise of satisfaction, Snickers encouraged repeat purchases and word of mouth recommendations.

Metrics: Customer lifetime value, repeat purchase rates, and brand advocacy metrics (such as Net Promoter Score) helped assess the effectiveness of Snickers' efforts in retaining customers and turning them into brand advocates.

Snickers' "You're Not You When You're Hungry" campaign effectively navigated the marketing funnel by leveraging humor, relatability, and emotional storytelling to drive awareness, engagement, and ultimately, sales. By understanding and addressing consumer needs at each stage of the funnel, Snickers succeeded in repositioning its brand and strengthening its connection with consumers.

The campaign's execution revolved around a series of television commercials, print advertisements, digital content, and social media engagement. Each advertisement depicted individuals acting out of character due to hunger, only to revert to their true selves after consuming a Snickers bar. These commercials featured various scenarios, including a diva throwing a tantrum, a football player performing poorly, and even a cowboy riding a tiny horse.

One of the campaign's key elements was the tagline: "You're Not You When You're Hungry." This simple yet impactful phrase became instantly recognizable and synonymous with Snickers. It was prominently featured in all advertisements, creating a cohesive brand message across different platforms.

In addition to traditional media, Snickers leveraged social media platforms such as Twitter and Facebook to further engage with consumers. They encouraged followers to share their own "hangry" moments using the hashtag #EatASNICKERS, fostering a sense of community and interaction around the campaign.

1. Creative Concept Development: The execution of Snickers' campaign began with the development of a creative concept centered around the theme "You're Not You When You're Hungry." Drawing on consumer insights and market research, the creative team at Snickers and its advertising agency, BBDO, conceptualized humorous scenarios that portrayed individuals behaving out of character due to hunger.

2. Television Commercials: The campaign's primary medium was television commercials, which featured a series of humorous vignettes depicting relatable situations where hunger leads to irrational behavior. Each commercial showcased a different scenario, such as a diva throwing a tantrum on set or an office worker transforming into a grumpy cat lady. These commercials effectively communicated the message that consuming a Snickers bar could restore normalcy and satisfaction.

3. Print Advertisements: In addition to television commercials, Snickers also executed the campaign through print advertisements in magazines, newspapers, and outdoor billboards. These print ads featured eye catching visuals and witty copy that reinforced the campaign's message of satisfying hunger with a Snickers bar. By leveraging a mix of visual and verbal cues, Snickers captured the attention of consumers in various offline channels.

4. Digital Content: Snickers extended the campaign's reach through digital channels, including social media platforms, online videos, and display ads. The brand created engaging digital content, such as short video clips and GIFs, that showcased the campaign's humor and relatability. Snickers encouraged user participation by launching interactive campaigns, such as "Hangry Moments" contests, where consumers could share their own stories of hunger induced antics.

5. Social Media Engagement: Snickers actively engaged with consumers on social media platforms like Twitter, Facebook, and Instagram, leveraging the campaign's tagline and hashtag #EatASNICKERS to spark conversations and drive engagement. The brand shared behind the scenes footage, memes, and user generated content to foster a sense of community and reinforce the campaign's message in a lighthearted and interactive manner.

6. Celebrity Endorsements and Partnerships: To further amplify the campaign's impact, Snickers collaborated with celebrities, athletes, and influencers who embodied the theme of "You're Not You When You're Hungry." These partnerships included endorsements from popular figures in sports, entertainment, and social media, who helped increase the campaign's visibility and credibility among their respective fan bases.

7. Integrated Marketing Campaign: Snickers executed an integrated marketing campaign that seamlessly integrated all elements across multiple channels and touchpoints. The brand ensured consistency in messaging, imagery, and tone across television, print, digital, and social media platforms, reinforcing the campaign's central theme and tagline to create a cohesive brand experience for consumers.

8. Continuous Optimization and Adaptation: Throughout the campaign, Snickers continuously monitored performance metrics and consumer feedback to optimize its execution strategy. The brand made adjustments in real time based on data insights, refining creative messaging, media placement, and audience targeting to maximize engagement and effectiveness. By remaining agile and responsive, Snickers ensured that its campaign remained relevant and impactful in a dynamic marketing landscape.

How the campaign was executed:

Snickers' strategy relied heavily on humor. They created a series of commercials featuring celebrities and everyday people who became unrecognizably cranky when hungry.

Early Days with Celebrity Power: The campaign kicked off with Alisters like Betty White and Willem Dafoe showcasing their "hangry" transformations. These humorous portrayals established the core message and grabbed audience attention.

Shifting Focus to Relatable Characters: As the campaign matured, celebrities became less prominent. The focus shifted to relatable scenarios with everyday people turning into outlandish characters when hungry. This broadened the appeal and made the situations more relatable.

Humor Across Platforms: The campaign wasn't limited to TV. Snickers embraced digital marketing, creating hilarious social media content, online games, and interactive experiences that mirrored the TV commercials.

The Power of Consistency:

Snickers maintained a consistent brand voice throughout the campaign. The tagline "You're Not You When You're Hungry" became a cultural touchstone. Visuals featured the instantly recognizable Snickers bar and the satisfying "snickers sound" became a signature element.

In conclusion, Snickers' execution of the "You're Not You When You're Hungry" campaign involved a multifaceted approach that combined creative storytelling, strategic media placement, digital engagement, and celebrity partnerships to effectively communicate the brand's message and drive consumer engagement and sales.

Campaign Challenges:

Despite the success of Snickers' "You're Not You When You're Hungry" campaign, several challenges and problems were encountered during its execution:

1. Balancing Humor with Sensitivity: One challenge for Snickers was striking the right balance between humor and sensitivity in portraying hunger induced behavior. While the campaign aimed to be humorous and relatable, there was a risk of inadvertently offending or trivializing individuals with genuine hunger related issues, such as food insecurity or eating disorders. Ensuring that the campaign remained lighthearted without being dismissive of these serious concerns required careful navigation.

2. Managing Consumer Expectations: The campaign's tagline, "You're Not You When You're Hungry," created high expectations among consumers regarding the transformative power of Snickers bars. Some consumers may have interpreted the campaign literally, expecting the product to have an immediate and dramatic effect on their mood and behavior. Managing these expectations and communicating the intended message of satisfying hunger in a playful manner was essential to prevent disappointment or backlash.

3. Avoiding Overexposure and Fatigue: With any long running advertising campaign, there is a risk of overexposure and audience fatigue. Snickers needed to carefully manage the frequency and distribution of campaign assets to prevent consumers from becoming desensitized to the message or perceiving it as repetitive. Introducing fresh creative concepts and periodically refreshing the campaign's imagery and messaging helped mitigate this risk.

4. Adapting to Cultural Sensitivities: Snickers operates in diverse global markets with varying cultural norms and sensitivities. Adapting the campaign's creative content to resonate with different cultural contexts while maintaining its core message posed a challenge. Certain cultural nuances or taboos related to food, humor, or advertising may have required adjustments to ensure the campaign's effectiveness and appropriateness across different regions.

5. Competing for Attention in a Crowded Market: The confectionery industry is highly competitive, with numerous brands vying for consumer attention and market share. Snickers faced the challenge of standing out amidst a crowded landscape of advertising messages and competing products. Maintaining relevance and differentiation in the face of evolving consumer preferences and emerging trends required ongoing innovation and strategic positioning.

6. Measuring Impact and ROI: Effectively measuring the impact and return on investment (ROI) of the campaign posed a challenge for Snickers. While metrics such as brand awareness, engagement, and sales growth provided valuable insights into the campaign's success, accurately attributing these outcomes to specific marketing activities could be complex. Snickers needed to employ robust analytics and attribution models to track the campaign's performance accurately and justify marketing expenditures.

While the campaign has been a resounding success, there are always challenges to consider:

- **Maintaining Freshness:** Keeping audiences engaged with a long running campaign requires constant innovation and fresh content creation. Snickers must avoid becoming predictable while staying true to the core message.
- **Cultural Sensitivity:** Humor can be subjective. Snickers must navigate cultural sensitivities to ensure the campaign continues to resonate with a global audience.
- **Evolving Media Landscape:** The media landscape is constantly changing. Snickers needs to adapt its strategy to stay relevant and connect with audiences on the platforms they use most.

Despite these challenges, Snickers' "You're Not You When You're Hungry" campaign demonstrated resilience and adaptability, successfully navigating potential pitfalls to become one of the most iconic and enduring advertising campaigns in recent memory.

The ad and catchy points:

Snickers' "You're Not You When You're Hungry" campaign featured a series of advertisements that humorously depicted individuals acting out of character due to hunger. Each ad presented a relatable scenario where someone's behavior was dramatically altered by hunger, only to return to normalcy after consuming a Snickers bar. These ads cleverly communicated the message that hunger can lead to mood swings and decreased performance, but Snickers can quickly satisfy hunger and restore individuals to their best selves.

Catchy Points in the Ads:

1. Celebrity Transformations:

One of the most memorable aspects of the ads was the use of well known personalities to illustrate the transformative power of Snickers. For example, an ad featured an irritable and diva like version of the iconic character Marilyn Monroe, who transforms back into her usual self after eating a Snickers bar. This celebrity cameo added an element of surprise and entertainment, capturing viewers' attention and making the ads highly shareable.

2. Humorous Situations:

The ads were filled with humor, presenting exaggerated and comical situations resulting from hunger induced mood swings. Whether it was a football player becoming a clumsy ballerina or a grumpy office worker morphing into a whistling construction worker, the scenarios were designed to elicit laughter and resonate with audiences who have experienced similar hunger related behavior changes.

3. Consistent Tagline:

The campaign's tagline, "You're Not You When You're Hungry," served as a unifying element across all ads. This catchy and memorable phrase effectively communicated the campaign's central message while creating a sense of continuity and recognition. By repeating the tagline in each ad, Snickers reinforced its association with satisfying hunger and returning individuals to their true selves.

4. Emotional Resonance:

Beyond the humor, the ads tapped into a deeper emotional truth – the feeling of relief and satisfaction that comes from satisfying hunger. Viewers could empathize with the characters' struggles and relate to the idea of hunger affecting mood and behavior. This emotional resonance helped forge a stronger connection between consumers and the Snickers brand.

5. Product Integration:

While the ads were humorous and entertaining, they also effectively showcased the product itself – the Snickers bar. The shots of individuals unwrapping and enjoying a Snickers bar served as a visual reminder of the solution to hunger induced mood swings, reinforcing the brand's positioning as a satisfying snack.

In summary, the catchy points in Snickers' "You're Not You When You're Hungry" ads included celebrity transformations, humorous situations, a consistent tagline, emotional resonance, and seamless product integration. These elements combined to create memorable and effective advertisements that not only entertained viewers but also effectively communicated Snickers' brand message and value proposition.

Key Elements and Messages Campaign:

1. **Tagline:** The central message of the campaign revolved around the iconic tagline: "You're Not You When You're Hungry." This tagline served as the anchor for all campaign communications, encapsulating the core insight that hunger can alter behavior and mood, and emphasizing the role of Snickers bars in restoring normalcy.
2. **Humorous Scenarios:** The campaign featured a series of humorous scenarios depicting individuals behaving out of character due to hunger. These scenarios ranged from a diva

throwing a tantrum to a football player performing poorly on the field. The exaggerated and absurd situations highlighted the absurdity of hunger induced behavior, eliciting laughter and recognition from viewers.

3. **Relatability:** Snickers capitalized on the universal experience of feeling "hangry" to create relatable content that resonated with consumers across demographics. By tapping into a shared human experience, the campaign fostered a sense of empathy and connection with the brand, making it memorable and engaging.

4. **Product Solution:** The campaign emphasized Snickers bars as the solution to hunger induced mood swings and cravings. Each advertisement showed individuals consuming a Snickers bar and quickly returning to their normal selves, highlighting the product's ability to satisfy hunger and restore energy levels.

5. **Cultural Relevance:** Snickers leveraged cultural references and timely events to enhance the campaign's relevance and appeal. The brand collaborated with celebrities, athletes, and influencers who embodied the theme of the campaign, further amplifying its message and reach among diverse audiences.

6. **Consistency Across Channels:** Snickers maintained consistency in messaging, imagery, and tone across all campaign channels, including television, print, digital, and social media. The tagline "You're Not You When You're Hungry" was prominently featured in all advertisements, creating a cohesive brand experience for consumers.

7. **Interactive Engagement:** Snickers encouraged consumer engagement through interactive campaigns and social media activations. The brand invited consumers to share their own "hangry" moments using the hashtag #EatASNICKERS, fostering a sense of community and participation around the campaign.

8. **Emotional Connection:** Beyond humor, the campaign aimed to create an emotional connection with consumers by tapping into feelings of empathy, understanding, and camaraderie. By acknowledging and validating the experience of feeling "hangry," Snickers positioned itself as a brand that understands and cares about its consumers' needs.

Overall, the key elements and messages of Snickers' "You're Not You When You're Hungry" campaign centered around humor, relatability, product efficacy, cultural relevance, and emotional connection, creating a memorable and impactful brand experience for consumers.

Platforms and channels:

Snickers' "You're Not You When You're Hungry" campaign utilized a variety of platforms and channels to reach its target audience and maximize engagement. These included:

1. **Television:** Television commercials were a primary platform for the campaign, allowing Snickers to reach a broad audience during popular programming slots. The humorous and attention grabbing commercials aired on both network and cable channels, ensuring widespread exposure.
2. **Print Media:** Print advertisements appeared in magazines, newspapers, and outdoor billboards, providing additional visibility for the campaign. Eye Catching visuals and witty copy reinforced the campaign's message and increased brand recall among print media consumers.
3. **Digital Platforms:** Snickers leveraged digital platforms such as websites, online videos, and display ads to extend the campaign's reach and engagement. Digital content allowed for interactive storytelling and user participation, driving further consumer interaction with the brand.
4. **Social Media:** Social media platforms played a crucial role in amplifying the campaign's message and fostering community engagement. Snickers maintained an active presence on platforms like Facebook, Twitter, and Instagram, sharing campaign content, engaging with followers, and encouraging user generated content using the hashtag #EatASNICKERS.
5. **YouTube:** Snickers uploaded campaign commercials and behind the scenes content to its YouTube channel, reaching a vast online audience and enabling easy sharing and virality. YouTube provided a platform for long form video content

and engagement with consumers through likes, comments, and shares.

6. **Events and Sponsorships:** Snickers capitalized on events and sponsorships to further promote the campaign and connect with consumers in person. The brand sponsored sports events, festivals, and other cultural gatherings, integrating campaign messaging into event activations and brand experiences.

7. **Influencer Partnerships:** Snickers collaborated with celebrities, athletes, and social media influencers who resonated with the campaign's target audience. These influencers helped amplify the campaign's message through their own social media channels, reaching new audiences and driving engagement with the brand.

8. **Point of Sale Marketing:** Snickers utilized point of sale marketing materials such as displays, signage, and promotions in retail stores and convenience outlets. These materials reinforced campaign messaging and encouraged impulse purchases at the point of sale.

By leveraging a diverse mix of platforms and channels, Snickers ensured that its "You're Not You When You're Hungry" campaign reached consumers wherever they consumed media, driving awareness, engagement, and ultimately, sales of Snickers bars.

Metrics for campaign:

The success of Snickers' "You're Not You When You're Hungry" campaign was measured using a range of key performance indicators (KPIs) to assess its impact on brand awareness, engagement, sales, and overall effectiveness. Some of the metrics used to evaluate the campaign included:

1. **Brand Awareness:**
   o **Brand Recall:** Measure of the percentage of consumers who correctly recall seeing or hearing Snickers' campaign advertisements.
   o **Brand Recognition:** Measure of the percentage of consumers who correctly identify Snickers as the brand

associated with the campaign's tagline, "You're Not You When You're Hungry."

2. **Engagement:**
   - **Social Media Engagement:** Metrics such as likes, shares, comments, and mentions on social media platforms like Facebook, Twitter, and Instagram user generated Content: Number of user generated posts and submissions using campaign hashtags (#EatASNICKERS) or related content.

3. **Sales and Revenue:**
   - **Sales Volume:** Measure of the increase in units sold of Snickers bars during the campaign period compared to baseline sales data.
   - **Revenue Growth:** Measure of the increase in revenue generated from sales of Snickers bars during the campaign period compared to previous periods.

4. **Consumer Perception:**
   - **Brand Sentiment:** Analysis of consumer sentiment towards Snickers and the campaign, gathered from social media mentions, online reviews, and surveys.
   - **Purchase Intent:** Measure of the percentage of consumers who express intent to purchase Snickers bars after exposure to the campaign.

5. **Digital Metrics:**
   - **Website Traffic:** Increase in website visits and page views on Snickers' official website as a result of campaign related content.
   - **Click Through Rate (CTR):** Measure of the percentage of users who click on digital ads or links to visit Snickers' website or engage with campaign content.

6. **Ad Effectiveness:**
   - **Ad Recall:** Measure of the percentage of consumers who remember seeing or hearing Snickers' campaign advertisements after a specified period.
   - **Ad Recognition:** Measure of the percentage of consumers who correctly identify Snickers as the brand associated with specific campaign advertisements.

7. **Return on Investment (ROI):**
   - **Cost per Acquisition (CPA):** Measure of the average cost incurred to acquire a new customer or generate a sale as a result of the campaign.
   - **Return on Ad Spend (ROAS):** Ratio of revenue generated from the campaign compared to the cost of advertising spend, expressed as a percentage.
8. **Industry Recognition:**
   - **Awards and Accolades:** Recognition received by the campaign from industry organizations, advertising competitions, and marketing publications, such as Cannes Lions, Effie Awards, and Adweek.

By tracking these metrics, Snickers was able to assess the effectiveness of its "You're Not You When You're Hungry" campaign, optimize marketing strategies, and justify investment in advertising initiatives.

Results:

While specific results with numbers for Snickers' "You're Not You When You're Hungry" campaign may not be available without access to proprietary data from Mars, Incorporated, I am sharing hypothetical examples of the type of results that the campaign might have achieved based on industry benchmarks and hypothetical scenarios:

1. **Brand Awareness:**
   - **Brand Recall:** 60% of consumers correctly recall seeing Snickers' campaign advertisements.
   - **Brand Recognition:** 50% of consumers correctly identify Snickers as the brand associated with the campaign's tagline.
2. **Engagement:**
   - **Social Media Engagement:** Snickers' campaign generates 100,000 likes, shares, and comments across social media platforms.

o **User generated Content:** Consumers create 5,000 posts and submissions using campaign hashtags (#EatASNICKERS) or related content.

3. **Sales and Revenue:**
   o **Sales Volume:** Snickers experiences a 20% increase in units sold of Snickers bars during the campaign period compared to baseline sales data.
   o **Revenue Growth:** Snickers achieves a 15% increase in revenue generated from sales of Snickers bars during the campaign period compared to previous periods.

4. **Consumer Perception:**
   o **Brand Sentiment:** 70% of consumer sentiment towards Snickers and the campaign is positive, based on analysis of social media mentions and online reviews.
   o **Purchase Intent:** 40% of consumers express intent to purchase Snickers bars after exposure to the campaign.

5. **Digital Metrics:**
   o **Website Traffic:** Snickers' official website experiences a 30% increase in website visits and page views as a result of campaign related content.
   o **Click through Rate (CTR):** Snickers achieves a 2% click through rate on digital ads and links to visit Snickers' website or engage with campaign content.

6. **Ad Effectiveness:**
   o **Ad Recall:** 70% of consumers remember seeing or hearing Snickers' campaign advertisements after a specified period.
   o **Ad Recognition:** 60% of consumers correctly identify Snickers as the brand associated with specific campaign advertisements.

7. **Return on Investment (ROI):**
   o **Cost per Acquisition (CPA):** Snickers incurs an average cost of $5 per new customer or generated sale as a result of the campaign.

Return on Ad Spend (ROAS): Snickers achieves a 300% return on ad spend, with revenue generated from the campaign being three times the cost of advertising spend.

8. **Industry Recognition:**
   - **Awards and Accolades:** Snickers' campaign receives multiple awards and accolades, including a Cannes Lions Gold Award and an Effie Award for marketing effectiveness.

These hypothetical results provide a snapshot of the potential impact and success of Snickers' "You're Not You When You're Hungry" campaign, demonstrating its effectiveness in driving brand awareness, engagement, sales, and overall marketing performance. Actual results may vary based on campaign execution, market conditions, and other factors.

Campaign Success Factors:

The success of Snickers' "You're Not You When You're Hungry" campaign can be attributed to several key factors:

1. **Clear and Memorable Messaging:** The campaign's tagline, "You're Not You When You're Hungry," was simple, memorable, and instantly recognizable. It effectively communicated the campaign's central message and resonated with consumers on a personal level, driving home the importance of satisfying hunger with Snickers bars.

2. **Humor and Relatability:** The campaign's humorous scenarios and relatable depictions of hunger induced behavior captured the attention of consumers and elicited laughter. By tapping into the universal experience of feeling "hangry," Snickers created an emotional connection with consumers, making the brand more relatable and approachable.

3. **Consistency Across Channels:** Snickers maintained consistency in messaging, imagery, and tone across all campaign channels, ensuring a cohesive brand experience for consumers. Whether through television commercials, print advertisements, digital content, or social media engagement, the campaign maintained a unified message that reinforced brand recall and recognition.

4. **Multi Channel Approach:** The campaign utilized a diverse mix of platforms and channels to reach consumers wherever they consumed media. From traditional television advertising to digital and social media activations, Snickers maximized its campaign's reach and engagement, ensuring broad exposure to its target audience.

5. **Engagement and Interaction:** Snickers encouraged consumer engagement and interaction with the campaign through social media activations, user generated content, and interactive campaigns. By inviting consumers to share their own "hangry" moments using campaign hashtags, Snickers fostered a sense of community and participation around the brand, driving further engagement and brand advocacy.

6. **Product Integration:** The campaign effectively integrated the Snickers product into its creative storytelling, highlighting the brand's role in satisfying hunger and restoring normalcy. By showcasing individuals consuming Snickers bars and experiencing immediate relief from hunger induced mood swings, the campaign reinforced the product's efficacy and benefits.

7. **Cultural Relevance:** Snickers leveraged cultural references and timely events to enhance the campaign's relevance and appeal. Collaborations with celebrities, athletes, and influencers further amplified the campaign's message and reach among diverse audiences, reinforcing Snickers' position as a culturally relevant and iconic brand.

8. **Measurement and Optimization:** Throughout the campaign, Snickers continuously monitored performance metrics and consumer feedback to optimize its strategy and execution. By tracking key performance indicators such as brand awareness, engagement, and sales impact, Snickers was able to refine its approach and maximize the campaign's effectiveness in real time.

Campaign Effectiveness: A Recipe for Success:

The results speak for themselves. Snickers' "You're Not You When You're Hungry" campaign has been a resounding success.

- **Sales & Market Share Boost:** Within a year, global sales increased by nearly 16%, demonstrating the campaign's effectiveness in driving brand preference and sales.
- **Award Winning Creativity:** The campaign garnered numerous awards, including Cannes Lions and Emmys, highlighting its creative excellence.
- **Cultural Phenomenon:** The campaign transcended advertising, becoming a part of pop culture. People use "hangry" in everyday conversations, solidifying the campaign's impact.

Key Ingredients of Success:

Several factors contributed to the campaign's enduring success:

- **Universal Appeal:** The campaign tapped into a relatable truth hunger's effect on mood and behavior. This resonated with a broad audience.
- **Humor as a Disarming Tactic:** Humor disarmed viewers, making the message more digestible and engaging. People enjoyed the exaggerated scenarios and laughed at themselves.
- **Celebrity Power & Relatable Characters:** Celebrities initially grabbed attention, while everyday people in later iterations ensured broader relatability.
- **Cross Platform Consistency:** The campaign's consistent message and visuals across platforms reinforced brand recognition and strengthened the core idea.
- **Long Term Commitment:** Snickers didn't abandon the campaign after initial success. They continue to create fresh content, keeping it relevant and engaging.

The Future of "You're Not You When You're Hungry":

Snickers' "You're Not You When You're Hungry" campaign is a testament to the power of humor and relatable storytelling in marketing. It's a case study that continues to inspire marketers today. As Snickers navigates the evolving media landscape, the campaign can be expected to adapt, finding new ways to connect with audiences and keep the "hangry" conversation going. Here are some potential areas for future development:

- **Interactive Experiences:** Snickers could leverage augmented reality or virtual reality to create immersive "hangry" experiences, further engaging the audience.
- **User generated Content:** Encouraging consumers to share their own "hangry" moments on social media could expand the campaign's reach and foster a sense of community.
- **Partnerships:** Collaborations with social media influencers, popular culture properties, or even fitness apps could explore new ways to connect with different demographics.

By incorporating these success factors into its "You're Not You When You're Hungry" campaign, Snickers was able to create a memorable and impactful marketing initiative that resonated with consumers worldwide, driving brand awareness, engagement, and sales growth.

Customer Reaction:

1. Customer reaction to Snickers' "You're Not You When You're Hungry" campaign was overwhelmingly positive, with the campaign resonating strongly with consumers across demographics. Here are some key aspects of customer reaction:
2. **Identification with the Message:** Many consumers identified with the campaign's central message that hunger can alter behavior and mood, leading to relatable and humorous situations. The tagline "You're Not You When

You're Hungry" struck a chord with individuals who had experienced "hangry" feelings themselves, leading to widespread recognition and appreciation of the campaign's relevance.

3. **Engagement on Social Media:** The campaign sparked significant engagement on social media platforms, with consumers sharing campaign content, participating in interactive campaigns, and contributing their own "hangry" moments using the campaign hashtag #EatASNICKERS. This social media activity created a sense of community and camaraderie around the brand, fostering further engagement and brand advocacy.

4. **Positive Brand Sentiment:** Customer sentiment towards Snickers and the campaign was overwhelmingly positive, with many expressing admiration for the brand's creative storytelling and humor. The campaign's ability to inject humor into everyday situations resonated with consumers, leading to increased brand affinity and loyalty.

5. **Increased Purchase Intent:** The campaign successfully influenced consumer behavior, with many expressing intent to purchase Snickers bars after exposure to the campaign. The humorous and relatable content showcased the product's benefits in satisfying hunger and restoring energy levels, leading to increased consideration and preference for Snickers among consumers.

6. **Viral Success:** Several elements of the campaign achieved viral success, with campaign commercials, digital content, and user generated memes being widely shared and discussed online. The campaign's ability to generate buzz and capture the attention of consumers contributed to its overall success and impact.

7. **Recognition and Awards:** Snickers' "You're Not You When You're Hungry" campaign received recognition and awards within the advertising industry, further validating its success and effectiveness. Awards such as Cannes Lions and Effie Awards underscored the campaign's creative excellence and marketing effectiveness, cementing its status as a standout advertising initiative.

Overall, customer reaction to Snickers' "You're Not You When You're Hungry" campaign was overwhelmingly positive, with consumers appreciating the campaign's humor, relatability, and effectiveness in communicating the brand's message. The campaign's ability to resonate with consumers on an emotional level and drive tangible business results solidified its status as one of the most memorable and impactful marketing campaigns in recent years.

Psychological reason for success:

The success of Snickers' "You're Not You When You're Hungry" campaign can be attributed to several psychological factors that resonated deeply with consumers:

1. **Emotional Connection:** The campaign tapped into consumers' emotions by addressing a universal experience: feeling "hangry" (hungry and angry). By acknowledging and validating this common feeling, Snickers created an emotional connection with consumers, who appreciated the brand's understanding of their everyday struggles.

2. **Humor and Relatability:** Humor is a powerful psychological tool that can create positive emotions and build rapport with an audience. The campaign's humorous scenarios and witty tagline elicited laughter and amusement, making the brand more relatable and likable to consumers. By presenting relatable situations where hunger induced behavior leads to comical outcomes, Snickers effectively captured consumers' attention and engagement.

3. **Social Proof:** The campaign leveraged social proof by showcasing individuals from different walks of life experiencing hunger induced mood swings and cravings. When consumers saw others sharing similar experiences, they were more likely to relate to the campaign and perceive Snickers as a solution to their own hunger related struggles. This sense of validation and social validation reinforced the campaign's effectiveness and resonated with consumers' desire for belonging and acceptance.

4. **Cognitive Dissonance:** The campaign played on the psychological principle of cognitive dissonance, which occurs when individuals experience conflicting thoughts, beliefs, or behaviors. The tagline "You're Not You When You're Hungry" created a sense of cognitive dissonance by highlighting the disparity between individuals' normal behavior and their behavior when hungry. By presenting Snickers bars as a solution to this dissonance, the campaign encouraged consumers to resolve their hunger induced discomfort by consuming the product.

5. **Brand Association:** Over time, Snickers has built a strong brand association with satisfaction and indulgence. The campaign reinforced this association by positioning Snickers bars as a satisfying and energizing snack option that could quickly curb hunger and restore normalcy. By leveraging existing brand perceptions and associations, Snickers effectively communicated its product benefits and differentiated itself from competitors.

Overall, the success of Snickers' "You're Not You When You're Hungry" campaign can be attributed to its ability to tap into consumers' emotions, leverage humor and relatability, and reinforce brand associations.

Business and Marketing lessons:

The success of Snickers' "You're Not You When You're Hungry" campaign offers several valuable business and marketing lessons:

1. **Understanding Consumer Psychology:** The campaign's success underscores the importance of understanding consumer psychology and emotions. By tapping into universal experiences like feeling "hangry," Snickers was able to create a campaign that resonated deeply with consumers, fostering emotional connections and driving brand loyalty.

2. **Humor as a Powerful Tool:** Humor can be a powerful tool for engaging consumers and creating memorable marketing campaigns. Snickers' use of humor in its campaign helped cut

through the clutter of advertising messages and capture consumers' attention, leading to increased brand recall and positive associations.

3. **Consistent Brand Messaging:** The campaign's consistent messaging across different channels and touchpoints contributed to its success. Snickers maintained a unified message centered around the tagline "You're Not You When You're Hungry," ensuring that consumers received a clear and cohesive brand experience regardless of where they encountered the campaign.

4. **Leveraging Cultural Relevance:** Snickers leveraged cultural relevance by incorporating timely references and collaborating with celebrities and influencers who resonated with its target audience. This helped the campaign stay relevant and engaging, further amplifying its impact and reach.

5. **Integrated Marketing Approach:** The campaign's use of a diverse mix of platforms and channels, including television, print, digital, and social media, demonstrated the power of an integrated marketing approach. By leveraging multiple channels to reach consumers wherever they consume media, Snickers maximized the campaign's effectiveness and engagement.

6. **Measuring Impact and Optimization:** Snickers continuously monitored performance metrics and consumer feedback to optimize its campaign strategy in real time. This emphasis on measurement and optimization allowed the brand to refine its approach and maximize the campaign's impact, driving tangible business results and ROI.

7. **Creating Brand Affinity:** The campaign's focus on building emotional connections with consumers helped create strong brand affinity and loyalty. By addressing consumers' needs and emotions in a relatable and authentic way, Snickers fostered lasting relationships with its audience, driving long term brand advocacy and sales.

Impact:

The "You're Not You When You're Hungry" campaign was an immense success for Snickers, achieving widespread recognition and driving significant increases in sales. The humorous and relatable nature of the advertisements resonated with consumers of all ages, leading to a surge in brand awareness and affinity.

The campaign also generated considerable buzz in the advertising industry, earning numerous awards and accolades for its creativity and effectiveness. It won multiple Cannes Lions awards, including the prestigious Grand Prix in the Film category. Additionally, it received praise for its innovative use of social media to extend the campaign's reach and engagement.

From a business perspective, Snickers experienced tangible results from the campaign. Sales of Snickers bars increased substantially during the campaign period and continued to grow in the years that followed. The brand's market share also expanded as it solidified its position as a leader in the confectionery industry.

The "You're Not You When You're Hungry" campaign has left a lasting legacy for Snickers, shaping the brand's identity and marketing strategy for years to come. The campaign's success demonstrated the power of humor and relatability in advertising, inspiring other brands to adopt similar approaches in their own campaigns.

Furthermore, the campaign's tagline has become ingrained in popular culture, referenced in memes, television shows, and everyday conversations. It has transcended its original context as a marketing slogan to become a cultural phenomenon, further cementing Snickers' status as an iconic brand.

Conclusion:

Snickers' "You're Not You When You're Hungry" campaign stands as a quintessential example of effective marketing and brand communication. Through a combination of humor, relatability, and emotional resonance, the campaign captured the attention and imagination of consumers worldwide, driving engagement, brand affinity, and sales. By understanding the psychological factors that influence consumer behavior and leveraging cultural relevance, Snickers created a campaign that transcended traditional advertising to become a cultural phenomenon.

The campaign's success was rooted in its ability to tap into universal human experiences, such as feeling "hangry," and present the Snickers brand as a solution to these relatable challenges. By maintaining consistent messaging across multiple channels and touchpoints, Snickers ensured a cohesive brand experience that resonated with consumers wherever they encountered the campaign.

Furthermore, Snickers' emphasis on measurement, optimization, and integrated marketing demonstrated a commitment to driving tangible business results and ROI. By continuously monitoring performance metrics and consumer feedback, Snickers was able to refine its strategy and maximize the campaign's impact, ultimately achieving significant increases in brand awareness, engagement, and sales.

Overall, Snickers' "You're Not You When You're Hungry" campaign serves as a testament to the power of understanding consumer psychology, leveraging humor and relatability, and adopting an integrated marketing approach to create lasting connections with consumers. As a result, the campaign has solidified Snickers' position as not only a beloved chocolate bar but also a cultural icon that understands and resonates with its audience on a deeply human level.

Snickers' "You're Not You When You're Hungry" campaign is a gold standard in marketing. It's a perfect storm of humor, relatable insights, and consistent execution. The campaign's success offers valuable lessons for marketers across industries. By understanding human behavior, tapping into universal truths, and leveraging humor effectively, brands can create campaigns that not only sell products but also become cultural touchstones.

This case study has explored the campaign's strategy, execution, impact, and lasting legacy. As Snickers continues to innovate and adapt, "You're Not You When You're Hungry" promises to remain a powerful marketing force for years to come.

Key Notes:

1. Celebrity Endorsements: The campaign leveraged well known personalities to illustrate the transformative effect of Snickers, adding an element of surprise and entertainment.

2. Humor and Relatability: Humorous scenarios showcased exaggerated situations resulting from hunger induced mood swings, resonating with audiences and eliciting laughter.

3. Consistent Tagline: The campaign's tagline, "You're Not You When You're Hungry," was memorable and effectively communicated Snickers' central message across all ads, ensuring brand recognition and recall.

4. Emotional Connection: Beyond humor, the ads tapped into deeper emotional truths, allowing viewers to empathize with the characters' struggles and relate to the idea of hunger affecting mood and behavior.

5. Product Integration: The ads seamlessly integrated shots of individuals enjoying Snickers bars, reinforcing the brand's positioning as a satisfying snack and offering a solution to hunger induced mood swings.

6. Entertainment Value: The ads were not only informative but also entertaining, ensuring that viewers remained engaged and interested in the campaign's message.

7. Share ability: The humorous and relatable nature of the ads made them highly shareable, amplifying the campaign's reach through word of mouth and social media sharing.

8. Consistency Across Channels: Snickers maintained consistency in messaging and imagery across various marketing channels, ensuring a cohesive brand experience for consumers.

9. Effectiveness in Driving Sales: The campaign's ability to capture attention, evoke emotions, and communicate the brand's value proposition contributed to its success in driving sales and market share growth.

10. Long Term Impact: By forging strong emotional connections with consumers and reinforcing its brand identity, Snickers laid the foundation for long term brand loyalty and advocacy.

2

NIKE'S "JUST DO IT" CAMPAIGN

Nike's "Just Do It" campaign emerged during a critical period for the athletic apparel giant. In the late 1980s, Nike faced intense competition from rival brands like Reebok, and its market share was under threat. To reinvigorate its brand identity and connect with consumers on a deeper level, Nike sought the expertise of advertising agency Wieden+Kennedy.

Wieden+Kennedy recognized the need for a campaign that would not only differentiate Nike from its competitors but also resonate with a broad audience. They embarked on a journey to distill Nike's essence into a simple, memorable message that encapsulated the brand's ethos of determination, resilience, and achievement.

The phrase "Just Do It" was inspired by the last words of Gary Gilmore, a convicted murderer executed in 1977. Dan Wieden, cofounder of Wieden+Kennedy, drew upon Gilmore's defiant statement as he faced his fate—a phrase that captured the spirit of seizing opportunities and overcoming obstacles without hesitation.

With this powerful slogan in hand, Nike launched its "Just Do It" campaign in 1988. The campaign featured a series of advertisements showcasing individuals from diverse backgrounds pushing their limits, pursuing their passions, and achieving success against all odds. From professional athletes to everyday people, Nike celebrated the human spirit in its myriad forms, inspiring viewers to embrace the "Just Do It" mentality in their own lives.

The campaign's success was immediate and profound. "Just Do It" became synonymous with Nike's brand identity, permeating popular culture and embedding itself in the collective consciousness of consumers worldwide. Its universal appeal transcended demographics, resonating with people of all ages, backgrounds, and athletic abilities.

Over the years, the "Just Do It" campaign evolved to reflect changing societal values and cultural dynamics. Nike embraced social causes and championed diversity, using its platform to advocate for gender equality, racial justice, and inclusivity. By staying relevant and addressing contemporary issues, Nike ensured that the "Just Do It" campaign remained a potent force in the world of marketing and beyond.

Today, decades after its inception, Nike's "Just Do It" campaign stands as a testament to the enduring power of a compelling message. It not only revitalized Nike's brand image but also inspired millions to embrace a mindset of determination, resilience, and relentless pursuit of excellence. As one of the most iconic and influential advertising campaigns of all time, "Just Do It" continues to shape the way we perceive Nike and ourselves, leaving an indelible mark on the landscape of marketing and popular culture.

Why the campaign was launched The Nike's Problem:

The launch of Nike's "Just Do It" campaign stemmed from a crucial problem faced by the company in the late 1980s: a need to revitalize its brand image and differentiate itself in a fiercely competitive market. At the time, Nike was facing stiff competition from rivals like Reebok and was struggling to maintain its market share and relevance.

Despite being a prominent player in the athletic apparel industry, Nike realized that it needed to connect with consumers on a deeper level beyond just selling products. There was a growing demand for brands that embodied values of determination, resilience, and achievement—qualities that resonated with individuals seeking to push beyond their limits and pursue their goals relentlessly.

In this context, Nike recognized the importance of repositioning itself and reshaping its brand identity to align with the aspirations and motivations of its target audience. The problem statement for the launch of the "Just Do It" campaign can be summarized as follows:

Nike needed to:

- Differentiate itself from competitors in a crowded market.
- Reinvigorate its brand image and appeal to consumers on a more emotional and personal level.
- Connect with individuals who sought inspiration, empowerment, and a sense of purpose beyond mere athletic performance.
- Cultivate a universal message that would resonate with a broad demographic, transcending age, gender, and athletic ability.
- Address shifting consumer preferences and societal values by embracing themes of inclusivity, diversity, and social activism.

In response to these challenges, Nike collaborated with advertising agency Wieden+Kennedy to develop a campaign that would capture the essence of its brand while inspiring consumers to embrace a mindset of determination, resilience, and relentless pursuit of excellence. Thus, the "Just Do It" campaign was conceived as a solution to reposition Nike in the hearts and minds of consumers, solidifying its status as a symbol of athletic prowess, personal empowerment, and unwavering determination.

Marketing Strategy:

Nike's "Just Do It" campaign was underpinned by a comprehensive marketing strategy aimed at redefining the brand's image, resonating with consumers on an emotional level, and solidifying its position as a leader in the athletic apparel industry. The marketing strategy encompassed several key elements:

- **Brand Positioning:** Nike positioned itself as more than just a seller of athletic shoes and apparel; it positioned itself as a champion of determination, resilience, and personal achievement. By aligning its brand with these values, Nike sought to differentiate itself from competitors and establish a deeper emotional connection with consumers.
- **Slogan Development:** The development of the iconic "Just Do It" slogan was central to the campaign's success. This simple yet powerful phrase encapsulated Nike's ethos and served as a rallying cry for individuals striving to overcome obstacles and pursue their goals. The slogan was versatile enough to resonate with a broad audience while embodying Nike's core values.
- **Inclusive Storytelling:** Nike adopted an inclusive approach to storytelling, featuring individuals from diverse backgrounds, professions, and athletic abilities in its advertisements. By showcasing real people facing real challenges, Nike appealed to a wide range of consumers and reinforced the message that determination knows no bounds.
- **Engaging Visuals:** The campaign utilized striking visuals and compelling narratives to capture viewers' attention and evoke emotion. Whether through print ads, television commercials, or digital content, Nike leveraged visually impactful imagery to convey the essence of the "Just Do It" mentality.
- **Athlete Endorsements:** While the campaign celebrated everyday individuals, Nike also leveraged endorsements from high profile athletes to lend credibility and prestige to its brand. By associating with elite athletes like Michael Jordan, Serena Williams, and Cristiano Ronaldo, Nike reinforced its

commitment to excellence and inspired consumers to aspire to greatness.

- **Multi Channel Approach:** Nike employed a Multi Channel marketing approach to reach consumers across various touchpoints. From traditional media outlets to digital platforms and social media channels, the campaign utilized a mix of advertising mediums to maximize exposure and engagement.
- **Social Cause Integration:** As the campaign evolved, Nike integrated social causes into its messaging, addressing issues such as gender equality, racial justice, and inclusivity. By aligning with these causes, Nike demonstrated its commitment to social responsibility and resonated with consumers who valued brands that stood for something beyond profit.
- **Continued Innovation:** Nike's marketing strategy prioritized innovation and creativity, constantly seeking new ways to captivate audiences and stay ahead of the competition. Whether through technological advancements in product design or immersive brand experiences, Nike remained at the forefront of marketing innovation.

In essence, Nike's "Just Do It" campaign was guided by a marketing strategy that combined authenticity, inclusivity, and storytelling prowess to inspire consumers and solidify the brand's position as a beacon of determination and achievement. By embracing these core principles and adapting to changing consumer preferences, Nike's marketing strategy has stood the test of time, leaving an indelible mark on the world of advertising and popular culture.

Marketing Research:

Nike's "Just Do It" campaign was backed by extensive marketing research aimed at understanding consumer preferences, attitudes, and behaviors. The research efforts were integral to shaping the campaign's messaging, targeting, and overall strategy. Here's how Nike conducted marketing research to support the "Just Do It" campaign:

- **Consumer Insight Gathering:** Nike conducted qualitative and quantitative research to gain deep insights into the mindset of its target audience. This included focus groups, surveys, interviews, and observational studies to understand consumers' motivations, aspirations, and pain points related to athletic performance and personal achievement.
- **Market Segmentation:** Nike segmented its target market based on demographics, psychographics, and behavioral factors. By identifying distinct consumer segments with unique needs and preferences, Nike could tailor its marketing messages and product offerings to resonate with each segment effectively.
- **Competitive Analysis:** Nike analyzed the strategies and positioning of its competitors to identify gaps and opportunities in the market. This involved studying competitor advertising campaigns, product offerings, pricing strategies, and brand messaging to inform Nike's own marketing approach and differentiate itself effectively.
- **Trend Analysis:** Nike monitored cultural trends, fashion trends, and shifts in consumer preferences to stay ahead of the curve and anticipate emerging opportunities. This included tracking social media conversations, monitoring industry publications, and collaborating with trend forecasting agencies to inform strategic decision making.
- **Brand Perception Studies:** Nike conducted brand perception studies to assess how consumers perceived the Nike brand compared to its competitors. This involved measuring brand awareness, brand associations, brand loyalty, and overall brand sentiment to identify areas for improvement and inform brand positioning strategies.
- **Product Testing and Feedback:** Nike solicited feedback from consumers through product testing and prototypes to ensure that its products met the needs and expectations of its target audience. This feedback loop helped Nike refine its product offerings and enhance customer satisfaction.
- **Digital Analytics:** Nike leveraged digital analytics tools to track online consumer behavior, website traffic, and engagement metrics. This data provided valuable insights

into how consumers interacted with Nike's digital platforms, allowing Nike to optimize its digital marketing efforts and improve the online customer experience.

- **Post Campaign Evaluation:** After launching the "Just Do It" campaign, Nike conducted Post Campaign evaluations to assess its effectiveness and impact. This involved measuring key performance indicators such as brand awareness, purchase intent, and consumer sentiment to gauge the campaign's success and identify areas for optimization in future marketing initiatives.

Buyer Persona:

For Nike's "Just Do It" campaign, creating detailed buyer personas was crucial for understanding and targeting the diverse audience that the campaign aimed to reach. Here's an example of a buyer persona tailored to the campaign:

Name: Sarah

Demographics:

- Age: 25-35
- Gender: Female
- Occupation: Marketing Manager
- Income: $50,000 $75,000 per year
- Location: Urban or suburban areas

Background:

Sarah is a young professional who leads a busy lifestyle balancing her career with personal interests. She is health conscious and enjoys staying active through activities like running, yoga, and gym workouts. Sarah is goal oriented and values self improvement both in her professional and personal life. She is socially conscious and supports brands that align with her values of inclusivity, empowerment, and sustainability.

Needs and Pain Points:

- **Motivation:** Sarah seeks motivation and inspiration to push beyond her limits and achieve her fitness and career goals.
- **Convenience:** With her busy schedule, Sarah values convenience and seeks products that fit seamlessly into her lifestyle.
- **Quality:** Sarah prioritizes quality and performance in the products she purchases, particularly in athletic apparel and footwear.
- **Identity:** Sarah uses her fashion choices to express her identity and values, preferring brands that resonate with her personal ethos.

Goals and Aspirations:

- **Improve Fitness:** Sarah aims to maintain an active lifestyle and improve her fitness levels through regular exercise and training.
- **Career Advancement:** Sarah is ambitious and aspires to advance in her career by excelling in her role and taking on new challenges.
- **Personal Growth:** Sarah is focused on personal development and seeks opportunities for learning, growth, and self improvement.

How Nike's "Just Do It" Campaign Resonates with Sarah:

- **Inspiration and Motivation:** The "Just Do It" campaign inspires Sarah to overcome obstacles and pursue her goals with determination and resilience.
- **Inclusivity and Empowerment:** The campaign's inclusive messaging resonates with Sarah's values of empowerment and inclusivity, making her feel represented and valued by the brand.
- **Performance and Quality:** Nike's reputation for high quality products reinforces Sarah's trust in the brand, assuring

her that Nike's apparel and footwear will support her active lifestyle and performance goals.

- **Brand Identity:** The "Just Do It" campaign aligns with Sarah's personal ethos and identity, making her proud to associate herself with the Nike brand and its message of empowerment and achievement.

Marketing Funnel:

Marketing Funnel Analysis for Nike's "Just Do It" Campaign:

The marketing funnel provides a framework for understanding the consumer journey from initial awareness to eventual conversion and advocacy. Analyzing how Nike's "Just Do It" campaign navigated this funnel sheds light on its effectiveness in driving brand engagement, consideration, and ultimately, sales.

Awareness Stage:

Objective: The primary goal at this stage was to generate widespread awareness of the "Just Do It" campaign and its empowering message.

Strategy: Nike utilized a mix of traditional and digital channels to reach a broad audience, including television commercials, print ads, social media, and influencer partnerships. The campaign's bold imagery and inspirational messaging captured attention and sparked curiosity among consumers.

Metrics: Key metrics at this stage included reach, impressions, and brand recall. Nike aimed to ensure that the "Just Do It" message resonated with consumers and left a lasting impression, laying the foundation for further engagement.

Interest and Consideration Stage:

- **Objective:** After capturing consumers' attention, the next step was to foster interest and consideration for Nike's products and brand values.

- **Strategy:** Nike focused on creating engaging content that showcased real athletes and their stories of perseverance and determination. This included compelling storytelling in television commercials, interactive digital experiences, and behind the scenes footage of athletes' training routines.
- **Metrics:** Metrics such as website traffic, social media engagement, and video views were important indicators of consumer interest and engagement with the campaign content. Nike aimed to deepen consumers' connection with the brand and inspire them to learn more about Nike's products and offerings.

Desire Stage:

- **Objective:** Once consumers were interested in the campaign, the goal was to stimulate desire and preference for Nike's products over competing brands.
- **Strategy:** Nike leveraged persuasive messaging and aspirational imagery to evoke emotions and reinforce its brand values of empowerment, determination, and excellence. The campaign highlighted the benefits of Nike products in helping athletes achieve their goals and overcome challenges.
- **Metrics:** Metrics such as brand sentiment, purchase intent, and consideration were used to gauge consumers' inclination towards Nike and their likelihood to choose Nike products over alternatives. Nike aimed to position itself as the preferred choice for athletes and active individuals seeking high performance sportswear and footwear.

Action Stage:

- **Objective:** The final stage of the funnel involved converting consumer interest and desire into action, i.e., purchasing Nike products.
- **Strategy:** Nike employed various tactics to facilitate the purchase process, including online sales promotions, retail partnerships, and product launches tied to the campaign. The campaign's memorable tagline, "Just Do It," served as a call

to action, prompting consumers to take the next step and make a purchase.

- **Metrics:** Sales data, conversion rates, and market share growth were key metrics used to measure the campaign's success in driving tangible business outcomes. Nike aimed to translate consumer engagement and preference into actual sales and revenue growth.

Retention and Advocacy:

- **Objective:** Beyond the initial purchase, Nike aimed to foster long term customer loyalty and advocacy.
- **Strategy:** Nike continued to engage with consumers through post purchase communications, loyalty programs, and community building initiatives. By delivering exceptional products and experiences, Nike aimed to turn satisfied customers into brand advocates who would recommend Nike to others and contribute to ongoing brand loyalty.
- **Metrics:** Metrics such as customer lifetime value, repeat purchase rates, and brand advocacy indicators (such as Net Promoter Score) helped assess Nike's success in retaining customers and fostering brand advocacy. Nike aimed to build lasting relationships with consumers and ensure their continued support and loyalty over time.

Nike's "Just Do It" campaign effectively navigated the marketing funnel by leveraging compelling storytelling, inspirational messaging, and strategic brand activations to drive awareness, engagement, consideration, and ultimately, sales. By understanding and addressing consumers' needs and aspirations at each stage of the funnel, Nike succeeded in building a strong emotional connection with its audience and driving tangible business results.

The catchy points in ads:

One of the most iconic ads associated with Nike's "Just Do It" campaign is the "Revolution" commercial, which aired in 1987, a year before the official launch of the campaign. This ad featured a young athlete in a deserted stadium, engaged in a solitary predawn training session. The athlete, later revealed to be a young basketball player named Michael Jordan, is seen pushing himself to the limit, practicing drills and perfecting his skills in the dimly lit arena.

The ad's narrative is simple yet powerful, capturing the essence of the "Just Do It" mentality. Here are some of the catchy points and key elements that made this ad resonate with audiences:

- **The Tagline:** "Just Do It" is a universal call to action. It's short, memorable, and avoids focusing on specific products, making it timeless.
- **Emotional Resonance:** The campaign went beyond showcasing athletic feats. It captured the emotions involved in pushing oneself, the struggle, the elation of achievement, and the sense of empowerment that comes from overcoming challenges. The ad evokes a sense of determination, dedication, and passion that transcends words. Viewers are drawn into the intense atmosphere of the deserted stadium, where the lone athlete demonstrates unwavering commitment to his craft. This emotional resonance taps into universal themes of perseverance and excellence, striking a chord with viewers on a profound level.
- **Visual Impact:** Ads featured evocative imagery and stories of athletes pushing their limits. From Michael Jordan's iconic slam dunks to everyday runners persevering through a tough race, the visuals showcased the power of dedication and achieving personal bests. The ad's cinematography is visually striking, with dramatic lighting and cinematic angles adding to the sense of intensity and urgency. The dimly lit stadium serves as a metaphorical backdrop for the athlete's journey, symbolizing the solitary pursuit of greatness and the sacrifices required to achieve it.

- **Soundtrack:** The ad is accompanied by the iconic track "Revolution" by The Beatles, which adds a sense of energy and momentum to the visuals. The song's driving beat and rebellious lyrics complement the theme of the ad, reinforcing the message of pushing boundaries and challenging the status quo.
- **Narrative Surprise:** The ad's reveal of Michael Jordan as the athlete adds an element of surprise and excitement, instantly capturing the audience's attention. Jordan's presence reinforces the ad's message of excellence and serves as a powerful endorsement of the Nike brand.
- **Universal Appeal:** While the ad features a high profile athlete like Michael Jordan, its message is universally relatable. Whether professional athletes or everyday individuals, viewers are inspired to embrace the "Just Do It" mentality and pursue their goals with relentless determination.

Overall, the "Revolution" commercial encapsulates the spirit of Nike's "Just Do It" campaign, inspiring audiences to push beyond their limits and seize opportunities with courage and conviction. Its emotional resonance, visual impact, and universal appeal make it a timeless masterpiece of advertising, embodying the core values of the Nike brand and leaving a lasting impression on viewers around the world.

Execution of Campaign:

The execution of Nike's "Just Do It" campaign was characterized by boldness, creativity, and a commitment to authenticity. Here's an overview of how the campaign was executed across various channels:

- **Advertising Campaigns:** Nike rolled out a series of compelling advertising campaigns featuring the "Just Do It" slogan. These campaigns showcased a diverse range of athletes, from professional sports stars to everyday individuals, demonstrating the universal applicability of the campaign's message. The advertisements were aired on television, featured in print media, and distributed across digital platforms to maximize reach and engagement.

- **Celebrity Endorsements:** Nike leveraged endorsements from high profile athletes such as Michael Jordan, Serena Williams, and LeBron James to lend credibility and prestige to the campaign. These athletes became synonymous with the "Just Do It" ethos, embodying the values of determination, resilience, and excellence that Nike sought to promote.

- **Social Media Activation:** Nike capitalized on the power of social media to amplify the "Just Do It" message and engage with consumers on a more personal level. The brand utilized platforms like Instagram, Twitter, and Facebook to share inspirational stories, behind the scenes content, and user generated content, fostering a sense of community and empowerment among its audience.

- **Event Sponsorship and Activation:** Nike sponsored major sporting events and competitions, leveraging these platforms to showcase its products and reinforce the "Just Do It" messaging. The brand also hosted experiential activations and popup events to engage with consumers directly, offering interactive experiences and exclusive product launches that further reinforced its brand identity.

- **Product Innovation:** Nike complemented its marketing efforts with innovative product launches designed to appeal to consumers' desire for performance, style, and innovation. The brand introduced new lines of athletic footwear, apparel, and accessories that embodied the spirit of the "Just Do It" campaign, incorporating cutting edge technologies and design elements to enhance performance and style.

- **Inclusive Messaging:** Nike embraced inclusivity and diversity in its marketing campaigns, featuring athletes from diverse backgrounds and abilities. This inclusive messaging resonated with consumers and underscored Nike's commitment to empowerment and equality.

- **Cause Marketing Initiatives:** As the campaign evolved, Nike integrated social and environmental causes into its messaging, addressing issues such as gender equality, racial justice, and sustainability. By aligning with these causes,

Nike demonstrated its commitment to social responsibility and resonated with consumers who valued brands that stood for something beyond profit.

The execution of Nike's "Just Do It" campaign was characterized by a Multi Channel approach that leveraged advertising, celebrity endorsements, social media, events, product innovation, and cause marketing initiatives to amplify the campaign's message and engage with consumers on a deeper level. Through its bold and creative execution, Nike succeeded in not only revitalizing its brand image but also inspiring millions to embrace the "Just Do It" mentality and pursue their goals with unwavering determination.

Campaign Challenges:

Despite its immense success, Nike's "Just Do It" campaign faced several challenges and problems along the way:

- **Controversial Endorsements:** While Nike's use of high profile athletes as endorsers contributed to the campaign's success, it also led to occasional controversies. For example, endorsements of athletes involved in scandals or controversial behavior could tarnish Nike's brand image and alienate consumers who valued integrity and ethical conduct.
- **Competition and Market Saturation:** The athletic apparel industry is highly competitive, with numerous brands vying for consumer attention. Maintaining market share and relevance in such a crowded landscape posed a continuous challenge for Nike, requiring the brand to continually innovate and differentiate itself from competitors.
- **Changing Consumer Preferences:** Consumer preferences and trends in fashion, fitness, and lifestyle evolve rapidly. Nike had to stay attuned to these shifts and adapt its marketing strategies and product offerings accordingly to remain relevant and resonate with its target audience.
- **Social and Political Backlash:** Nike's integration of social and political themes into its marketing campaigns, such as addressing issues of racial injustice or gender equality, sometimes sparked backlash from certain segments of the

population. Balancing the brand's commitment to social responsibility with the risk of alienating conservative consumers posed a delicate challenge for Nike.

- **Counterfeiting and Brand Protection:** Nike's iconic branding and popularity made it a target for counterfeiters, resulting in significant revenue losses and damage to the brand's reputation. Nike had to invest resources in brand protection efforts to combat counterfeiting and protect its intellectual property rights.
- **Supply Chain Issues:** Nike's global supply chain, which involves sourcing materials and manufacturing products in various countries, presented challenges related to labor practices, environmental sustainability, and logistical efficiency. Ensuring ethical and sustainable practices throughout the supply chain while maintaining cost effectiveness and quality control was a complex and ongoing challenge for the company.
- **Adapting to Digital Transformation:** The rise of ecommerce and digital marketing posed both opportunities and challenges for Nike. While digital channels offered new avenues for reaching consumers and engaging with them directly, they also required Nike to adapt its marketing strategies and invest in technology and digital infrastructure to remain competitive in the digital age.

Despite these challenges, Nike's "Just Do It" campaign has demonstrated remarkable resilience and adaptability, evolving over the years to address emerging trends and navigate complex issues while remaining true to its core values and inspiring millions around the world to "Just Do It."

Campaign Objectives:

The objectives of Nike's "Just Do It" campaign were multifaceted, reflecting the brand's desire to achieve various strategic goals and connect with consumers on a deeper level. Here are the primary campaign objectives:

- **Repositioning the Brand:** Nike aimed to reposition itself in the minds of consumers, shifting from being solely a seller of athletic products to a provider of inspiration, empowerment, and motivation. The campaign sought to elevate Nike's brand image beyond just sportswear and position it as a symbol of determination, resilience, and achievement.
- **Differentiation from Competitors:** In a crowded marketplace with fierce competition from brands like Adidas and Reebok, Nike sought to differentiate itself by leveraging its unique brand identity and values. The "Just Do It" campaign aimed to set Nike apart from competitors by emphasizing its commitment to pushing boundaries, defying limitations, and embracing the challenges of life.
- **Inspiring Consumer Engagement:** Nike aimed to inspire and engage consumers on an emotional level, encouraging them to adopt the "Just Do It" mentality in their own lives. By showcasing real stories of perseverance, triumph, and personal growth, the campaign sought to foster a sense of connection and resonance with consumers, driving brand loyalty and affinity.
- **Expanding Target Audience:** While Nike had traditionally targeted athletes and sports enthusiasts, the "Just Do It" campaign aimed to broaden its appeal and reach a wider demographic. By featuring individuals from diverse backgrounds and professions, the campaign appealed to a broader audience, including non athletes and everyday individuals seeking motivation and inspiration.
- **Driving Sales and Revenue:** Ultimately, Nike's overarching objective was to drive sales and revenue growth by increasing brand awareness, enhancing brand perception, and strengthening consumer loyalty. The campaign aimed to

translate the emotional connection forged through its messaging into tangible business outcomes, driving consumer engagement and purchase intent.

- **Social Impact and Influence:** Beyond business objectives, the "Just Do It" campaign also aimed to make a positive social impact and influence societal attitudes and behaviors. By addressing themes of inclusivity, empowerment, and social justice, Nike sought to use its platform to spark conversations, raise awareness, and inspire positive change in the world.

Nike's "Just Do It" campaign was driven by a combination of brand building, consumer engagement, and social impact objectives, all aimed at reinforcing Nike's position as a leader in the athletic apparel industry while inspiring individuals to pursue their goals with courage, determination, and resilience.

Key Elements and Messages:

The success of Nike's "Just Do It" campaign can be attributed to its compelling messaging and key elements that resonated with consumers on a profound level. Here are the key elements and messages that defined the campaign:

- **Slogan: "Just Do It":** The campaign's iconic slogan encapsulated the essence of Nike's ethos, urging consumers to push beyond their limits and pursue their goals relentlessly. It conveyed a sense of empowerment, encouraging individuals to take action and overcome obstacles with determination and resilience.
- **Inspirational Storytelling:** Nike utilized powerful storytelling to convey its message of determination and achievement. The campaign featured real stories of athletes and individuals overcoming challenges, defying odds, and achieving success through sheer perseverance and dedication. These stories inspired viewers and reinforced the campaign's message of empowerment and resilience.

- **Inclusive Representation:** The campaign celebrated diversity and inclusivity by featuring individuals from various backgrounds, professions, and athletic abilities. By showcasing a diverse range of people pursuing their passions and dreams, Nike emphasized that the "Just Do It" mentality is accessible to everyone, regardless of age, gender, or background.

- **Emotional Resonance:** Nike's messaging evoked strong emotions, tapping into universal themes of perseverance, determination, and triumph. Whether through stirring visuals, compelling narratives, or inspirational music, the campaign connected with viewers on an emotional level, forging a deep and lasting bond with the brand.

- **Celebrity Endorsements:** Nike leveraged endorsements from high profile athletes such as Michael Jordan, Serena Williams, and LeBron James to lend credibility and prestige to the campaign. These athletes served as powerful ambassadors for the "Just Do It" mentality, embodying the values of excellence, resilience, and relentless pursuit of greatness.

- **Social and Cultural Relevance:** Nike addressed contemporary social and cultural issues in its messaging, aligning the campaign with broader societal conversations around topics such as gender equality, racial justice, and inclusivity. By taking a stand on these issues, Nike demonstrated its commitment to social responsibility and resonated with consumers who valued brands that stood for something beyond profit.

- **Urgency and Action:** The campaign's messaging conveyed a sense of urgency and action, encouraging viewers to seize opportunities and pursue their goals with conviction. Whether through calls to Action or motivational slogans, Nike inspired individuals to embrace the "Just Do It" mentality and take bold steps towards realizing their dreams.

The empowerment, resilience, inclusivity, and social impact, resonating with consumers around the world and solidifying Nike's position as a cultural icon and a beacon of inspiration for generations to come. The key elements and messages of Nike's 'Just Do It' campaign emphasized.

Platforms and channels:

Nike's "Just Do It" campaign utilized a variety of platforms and channels to reach and engage with its target audience. Here are some of the key platforms and channels through which the campaign was executed:

- **Television Commercials:** Nike aired television commercials featuring the "Just Do It" messaging on both broadcast and cable networks. These commercials often featured high production value visuals, compelling storytelling, and endorsements from celebrity athletes, capturing the attention of viewers and reinforcing the campaign's message of determination and achievement.
- **Print Advertising:** Nike placed print advertisements in magazines, newspapers, and outdoor billboards to extend the reach of the "Just Do It" campaign. These print ads often featured bold visuals, inspirational slogans, and endorsements from athletes, effectively conveying the brand's message to consumers in various print media outlets.
- **Digital Marketing:** Nike leveraged digital marketing channels such as its website, social media platforms, and email newsletters to amplify the "Just Do It" campaign. The brand created engaging content, including videos, blog posts, and interactive experiences, to connect with consumers online and foster a sense of community around the campaign's message.
- **Social Media:** Nike utilized social media platforms such as Instagram, Twitter, Facebook, and YouTube to engage with consumers and amplify the "Just Do It" messaging. The brand shared inspirational stories, behind the scenes content, user generated content, and interactive challenges to spark conversations and encourage audience participation.

- **Athlete Endorsements:** Nike leveraged endorsements from high profile athletes to extend the reach and impact of the "Just Do It" campaign. Athletes such as Michael Jordan, Serena Williams, LeBron James, and Cristiano Ronaldo served as powerful ambassadors for the campaign, sharing their own stories of perseverance and success and inspiring millions of fans around the world.
- **Events and Sponsorships:** Nike sponsored major sporting events, competitions, and cultural festivals to showcase its products and reinforce the "Just Do It" messaging. The brand hosted experiential activations, pop up shops, and athlete meet and greets to engage with consumers directly and create memorable brand experiences.
- **Retail Partnerships:** Nike collaborated with retail partners and distributors to promote the "Just Do It" campaign in store and online. The brand created co branded displays, promotions, and exclusive product launches to drive foot traffic and sales at retail locations and ecommerce platforms.

Metrics for campaign:

Metrics for evaluating the success of Nike's "Just Do It" campaign can encompass a range of key performance indicators (KPIs) across various stages of the marketing funnel. Here are some metrics that Nike might have used to measure the effectiveness of the campaign:

1. **Brand Awareness:**
   o **Reach:** Measure the total number of people exposed to the campaign through various channels, including television, digital, and print.
   o **Impressions:** Track the total number of times the campaign content was viewed or displayed to individuals.
   o **Social media mentions:** Monitor the volume of mentions, shares, and interactions related to the campaign on social media platforms.

2. **Engagement:**
   o **Click through rate (CTR):** Measure the percentage of people who clicked on campaign content, such as ads, emails, or social media posts, to visit Nike's website or landing pages.
   o **Social media engagement:** Track likes, comments, shares, and other interactions with campaign related content on social media platforms.
   o **Time spent on site:** Analyze the average duration visitors spend on Nike's website or campaign specific landing pages to gauge engagement levels.
3. **Consumer Perception:**
   o **Brand sentiment analysis:** Assess the sentiment of consumer conversations and mentions related to the campaign on social media and other online platforms.
   o **Surveys and focus groups:** Gather feedback from consumers through surveys, interviews, or focus groups to understand their perceptions and attitudes towards the campaign and the Nike brand.
4. **Conversion:**
   o **Conversion rate:** Measure the percentage of website visitors who completed a desired action, such as making a purchase, signing up for a newsletter, or downloading a resource.
   o **Sales revenue:** Track the total revenue generated from campaign related purchases or conversions, both online and offline.
   o **Coupon redemptions:** Monitor the number of coupons or promotional codes redeemed by consumers in response to the campaign.
5. **Retention and Loyalty:**
   o **Customer retention rate:** Measure the percentage of customers who continue to engage with Nike and make repeat purchases over a specified period.
   o **Customer lifetime value (CLV):** Calculate the total value that a customer contributes to Nike over their entire relationship with the brand, including purchases, referrals, and loyalty program participation.

6. **Social Impact and Advocacy:**
   o **Social causes impact:** Assess the impact of the campaign's messaging on social causes and issues, such as gender equality, racial justice, and sustainability.
   o **Brand advocates:** Identify and measure the influence of brand advocates and ambassadors who actively promote the campaign and the Nike brand within their networks.

By tracking these metrics, Nike can evaluate the effectiveness of its "Just Do It" campaign, identify areas for optimization, and measure the campaign's impact on brand awareness, engagement, conversion, and long term customer loyalty.

Results

While specific results and numbers for Nike's "Just Do It" campaign may not be publicly available, we can speculate on potential outcomes based on industry standards and the campaign's widespread impact. Here's a hypothetical breakdown of potential results with numbers:

1. **Brand Awareness:**
   o **Reach:** The campaign reached millions of consumers globally through various channels, with estimates suggesting a reach of over 100 million individuals.
   o **Impressions:** The campaign generated billions of impressions across television, digital, and print media, with an estimated impression count exceeding 5 billion.
2. **Engagement:**
   o **Click through rate (CTR):** The campaign achieved a strong CTR of around 2% for digital ads, indicating high levels of engagement with campaign content.
   o **Social media engagement:** Nike's campaign generated significant social media engagement, with posts receiving thousands of likes, shares, and comments across platforms.

3. **Consumer Perception:**
   o **Brand sentiment analysis:** Sentiment analysis of consumer conversations showed overwhelmingly positive sentiment towards the campaign, with over 80% of mentions expressing favorable opinions.
   o **Surveys and focus groups:** Consumer surveys indicated high levels of brand favorability and resonance with the campaign message, with over 70% of respondents reporting increased affinity for the Nike brand.
4. **Conversion:**
   o **Conversion rate:** The campaign drove a conversion rate of approximately 5% for online purchases, exceeding industry benchmarks for similar campaigns.
   o **Sales revenue:** Nike's "Just Do It" campaign generated over $500 million in incremental sales revenue during the campaign period, representing a significant uplift in revenue.
5. **Retention and Loyalty:**
   o **Customer retention rate:** Nike experienced a 10% increase in customer retention rates among consumers exposed to the campaign, indicating enhanced loyalty and repeat purchases.
   o **Customer lifetime value (CLV):** The CLV of customers engaged with the campaign increased by 15%, driven by higher purchase frequency and average order value.
6. **Social Impact and Advocacy:**
   o **Social causes impact:** The campaign's messaging around social causes led to increased awareness and engagement with issues such as gender equality and racial justice, with over 60% of consumers expressing support for Nike's stance on these issues.
   o **Brand advocates:** The campaign cultivated a community of brand advocates and ambassadors who actively promoted Nike's message, resulting in a 20% increase in referral traffic and word of mouth recommendations.

These hypothetical results illustrate the potential impact and effectiveness of Nike's "Just Do It" campaign in driving brand awareness, engagement, conversion, and advocacy. While actual results may vary, such outcomes would represent a significant success for the campaign and reinforce Nike's position as a leader in the athletic apparel industry.

Campaign Success Factors:

The success of Nike's "Just Do It" campaign can be attributed to several key factors that contributed to its effectiveness in resonating with consumers and achieving its objectives. Here are the campaign success factors:

- **Compelling Messaging:** The campaign's iconic slogan, "Just Do It," encapsulated Nike's ethos of determination, resilience, and achievement in just three words. This simple yet powerful message resonated with consumers on a deep emotional level, inspiring them to overcome obstacles and pursue their goals with unwavering conviction.
- **Authentic Storytelling:** Nike's use of authentic storytelling featuring real athletes and individuals from diverse backgrounds lent credibility and relatability to the campaign. By sharing compelling stories of perseverance, triumph, and personal growth, Nike connected with consumers on a human level, fostering a sense of empathy and inspiration.
- **Inclusive Representation:** The campaign celebrated diversity and inclusivity by featuring athletes and individuals of all ages, genders, and abilities. This inclusive representation not only reflected the diverse demographics of Nike's audience but also reinforced the brand's commitment to empowerment and equality.
- **High profile Endorsements:** Nike's collaboration with high profile athletes such as Michael Jordan, Serena Williams, and LeBron James lent credibility, prestige, and aspirational appeal to the campaign. These endorsements helped elevate the campaign's visibility and reach while reinforcing Nike's association with excellence and achievement.

- **Multi Channel Approach:** Nike utilized a Multi Channel marketing approach to maximize the campaign's reach and engagement across various touchpoints. From television commercials and print advertisements to digital platforms and social media, Nike ensured that the "Just Do It" message was omnipresent, enabling it to connect with consumers wherever they were.
- **Emotional Resonance:** The campaign evoked strong emotions, tapping into universal themes of perseverance, determination, and triumph. Whether through stirring visuals, compelling narratives, or inspirational music, Nike's messaging struck a chord with consumers, fostering a deep emotional connection and leaving a lasting impression.
- **Social Impact and Advocacy:** By integrating social and cultural themes into its messaging, Nike demonstrated its commitment to social responsibility and activism. The campaign's alignment with issues such as gender equality, racial justice, and sustainability resonated with socially conscious consumers, further enhancing the brand's relevance and appeal.
- **Continuous Innovation:** Nike's willingness to innovate and evolve its marketing strategies ensured that the "Just Do It" campaign remained fresh, relevant, and impactful over time. Whether through technological advancements, creative collaborations, or cultural insights, Nike continued to push boundaries and stay ahead of the curve in the ever changing landscape of marketing and advertising.

The success of Nike's "Just Do It" campaign can be attributed to its compelling messaging, authentic storytelling, inclusive representation, high profile endorsements, Multi Channel approach, emotional resonance, social impact, and continuous innovation. By leveraging these key factors, Nike succeeded in inspiring millions around the world to embrace the "Just Do It" mentality and pursue their goals with courage, determination, and resilience.

Customer Reaction:

The customer reaction to Nike's "Just Do It" campaign was overwhelmingly positive and contributed significantly to its success. Here are some common reactions and responses from customers:

- **Inspiration and Motivation:** Many customers found the campaign to be highly inspirational and motivational, with the "Just Do It" messaging resonating deeply with their personal aspirations and goals. The campaign's emphasis on determination, resilience, and overcoming obstacles inspired individuals to push beyond their limits and pursue their dreams with renewed vigor and conviction.
- **Emotional Connection:** Nike's authentic storytelling and inclusive representation fostered a strong emotional connection with customers. By featuring real stories of athletes and individuals overcoming challenges, the campaign touched the hearts of viewers and elicited feelings of empathy, empowerment, and solidarity.
- **Brand Loyalty and Affinity:** The "Just Do It" campaign reinforced Nike's position as a brand synonymous with excellence, achievement, and empowerment. Customers who resonated with the campaign's message felt a deeper sense of loyalty and affinity towards the Nike brand, viewing it not just as a provider of athletic apparel but as a source of inspiration and motivation in their lives.
- **Social Advocacy**: Nike's integration of social and cultural themes into the campaign resonated with socially conscious customers, who appreciated the brand's commitment to addressing issues such as gender equality, racial justice, and inclusivity. Many customers applauded Nike for using its platform to spark meaningful conversations and advocate for positive social change.
- **Increased Engagement:** The campaign generated significant engagement and interaction from customers across various channels, including social media, online forums, and community events. Customers actively shared campaign

content, participated in discussions, and expressed their support for the campaign's message, amplifying its reach and impact.

- **Purchase Intent:** The positive customer reaction to the "Just Do It" campaign translated into increased purchase intent and sales for Nike. Customers who felt inspired and motivated by the campaign were more likely to consider Nike products for their athletic and lifestyle needs, driving business growth and revenue for the brand.

The customer reaction to Nike's "Just Do It" campaign was overwhelmingly positive, with many individuals feeling inspired, empowered, and motivated to embrace the campaign's message of determination and resilience in their own lives. By resonating deeply with customers on both an emotional and aspirational level, the campaign solidified Nike's position as a leader in the athletic apparel industry and left a lasting impression on consumers around the world.

Psychological Reason for success:

The success of Nike's "Just Do It" campaign can be attributed to several psychological factors that resonated with consumers and elicited strong emotional responses. Here are some key psychological reasons for the campaign's success:

- **Sense of Empowerment:** The "Just Do It" campaign empowered consumers by instilling a sense of self efficacy and agency. The slogan encouraged individuals to take action and pursue their goals with confidence, reinforcing the belief that they have the ability to overcome challenges and achieve success.
- **Inspirational Role Models:** By featuring real stories of athletes and individuals overcoming obstacles, the campaign provided consumers with relatable role models to look up to. These stories inspired admiration, emulation, and a sense of identification, motivating individuals to strive for greatness in their own lives.

- **Social Proof:** The use of high profile athletes and celebrities as endorsers provided social proof of the campaign's message. Consumers were more likely to trust and emulate the behaviors of admired athletes, leading to increased engagement and adoption of the "Just Do It" mentality.
- **Emotional Connection:** Nike's storytelling evoked strong emotional responses from consumers, tapping into universal emotions such as determination, resilience, and triumph. The campaign's emotive content fostered a deep emotional connection with viewers, enhancing brand loyalty and affinity.
- **Cognitive Dissonance Reduction:** The campaign helped consumers reduce cognitive dissonance by aligning their beliefs and values with the brand's message. Individuals who aspired to be active, determined, and successful found validation and reinforcement in the campaign, reducing any internal conflicts and reinforcing their positive perceptions of Nike.
- **Aspirational Identity:** The campaign appealed to consumers' desire for self improvement and personal growth by associating the Nike brand with aspirational qualities such as excellence, achievement, and perseverance. By adopting Nike products and embodying the "Just Do It" mentality, consumers could enhance their self image and project a more empowered and confident identity.
- **Fear of Missing Out (FOMO):** The campaign leveraged FOMO by creating a sense of urgency and opportunity around seizing the moment and taking action. Consumers who identified with the campaign's message feared missing out on opportunities for growth and success if they did not embrace the "Just Do It" mentality.

Nike's "Just Do It" campaign appealed to consumers' psychological needs for empowerment, inspiration, belonging, and self expression, creating a powerful emotional connection that drove engagement, loyalty, and advocacy for the brand. By tapping into these psychological drivers, Nike succeeded in creating a campaign that resonated deeply with consumers and left a lasting impact on their perceptions and behaviors.

Business and Marketing lessons:

Nike's "Just Do It" campaign offers several valuable business and marketing lessons that can be applied by companies seeking to create impactful and successful campaigns. Here are some key lessons:

- **Embrace a Powerful Message:** The campaign's iconic slogan, "Just Do It," encapsulates a simple yet powerful message that resonates with consumers on an emotional level. Lesson: Craft a clear and compelling message that speaks to your brand's values and resonates with your target audience.
- **Leverage Authentic Storytelling:** Nike's use of authentic storytelling featuring real athletes and individuals from diverse backgrounds lent credibility and relatability to the campaign. Lesson: Share authentic stories that humanize your brand and connect with consumers on a personal level.
- **Harness the Power of Inspiration:** The campaign inspired and motivated consumers to overcome obstacles and pursue their goals with determination and resilience. Lesson: Create content that inspires and empowers your audience, fostering a positive emotional connection with your brand.
- **Cultivate Brand Ambassadors:** Nike's collaboration with high profile athletes served as powerful endorsements that lent credibility and aspirational appeal to the campaign. Lesson: Identify and cultivate brand ambassadors who embody your brand's values and resonate with your target audience.
- **Embrace Diversity and Inclusivity:** The campaign celebrated diversity and inclusivity by featuring athletes and individuals from various backgrounds, reflecting Nike's commitment to empowerment and equality. Lesson: Embrace diversity and inclusivity in your marketing efforts, ensuring that your brand is accessible and relatable to a wide range of consumers.

- **Utilize a Multi Channel Approach:** Nike utilized a Multi Channel marketing approach to maximize the campaign's reach and engagement across various touchpoints. Lesson: Leverage multiple channels, including television, digital, social media, and events, to amplify your message and connect with consumers wherever they are.
- **Drive Social Impact:** Nike's integration of social and cultural themes into the campaign resonated with socially conscious consumers and sparked meaningful conversations. Lesson: Align your brand with social causes and issues that matter to your audience, demonstrating your commitment to making a positive impact on society.
- **Continuous Innovation:** Nike's willingness to innovate and evolve its marketing strategies ensured that the "Just Do It" campaign remained fresh, relevant, and impactful over time. Lesson: Stay ahead of the curve by continuously innovating and adapting your marketing efforts to meet the evolving needs and preferences of your audience.

Legacy:

The enduring legacy of Nike's "Just Do It" campaign transcends the realm of marketing to become a cultural icon and a symbol of inspiration and empowerment. Since its inception in 1988, the campaign has left an indelible mark on the collective consciousness, shaping not only the trajectory of the Nike brand but also influencing attitudes and behaviors around the world.

At its core, the legacy of the "Just Do It" campaign lies in its ability to inspire individuals to push beyond their limits and pursue their dreams with unwavering determination. The campaign's iconic slogan has become more than just a marketing tagline; it has evolved into a mantra for success, motivating millions to overcome obstacles, defy expectations, and achieve greatness in all aspects of life.

Moreover, the campaign's enduring legacy is evident in its impact on popular culture and societal norms. The "Just Do It" mentality has permeated various facets of society, from sports and fitness to business and personal development. Its message of empowerment and resilience has inspired countless individuals to embrace challenges, take risks, and seize opportunities with courage and conviction.

Furthermore, the campaign's legacy is reflected in Nike's continued commitment to social responsibility and advocacy. By aligning with social causes and addressing issues such as gender equality, racial justice, and environmental sustainability, Nike has demonstrated its role as a catalyst for positive change in the world. The brand's willingness to use its platform to spark conversations and drive meaningful impact underscores the enduring relevance and impact of the "Just Do It" campaign.

The enduring legacy of Nike's "Just Do It" campaign lies in its ability to inspire, empower, and create positive change in the world. From its iconic slogan to its authentic storytelling and social impact, the campaign has left an indelible mark on the hearts and minds of millions, shaping attitudes, behaviors, and aspirations for generations to come. As a cultural icon and symbol of empowerment, the "Just Do It" campaign continues to inspire individuals to embrace their potential, chase their dreams, and "just do it."

Nike's "Just Do It" campaign has transcended borders and cultures to become a global phenomenon, resonating with individuals from diverse backgrounds and inspiring them to embrace the campaign's message of determination, resilience, and achievement.

From the bustling streets of New York City to the remote villages of Africa, the "Just Do It" mentality has taken root, empowering individuals to push beyond their limitations and pursue their goals with unwavering conviction. Across continents and languages, the campaign's iconic slogan has become a universal symbol of empowerment, uniting people around the world in a shared pursuit of excellence and success.

The global reach of the "Just Do It" campaign is evident in its widespread adoption and recognition across international markets. Whether through television commercials, digital advertising, or social media engagement, Nike has successfully extended the campaign's reach to every corner of the globe, reinforcing its position as a cultural icon and a beacon of inspiration for millions.

Moreover, the campaign's impact extends beyond just marketing success; it has become a cultural touchstone that transcends geographic boundaries and societal norms. The "Just Do It" mentality has inspired individuals from diverse cultures and backgrounds to overcome adversity, break barriers, and achieve greatness in their own lives, regardless of their circumstances.

In essence, Nike's "Just Do It" campaign represents more than just a marketing strategy; it embodies a universal ethos that speaks to the human spirit and transcends cultural differences. As a global phenomenon, the campaign continues to inspire individuals around the world to embrace their potential, chase their dreams, and "just do it," wherever they may be.

Nike's "Just Do It" campaign has extended far beyond the realm of fitness, evolving into a global cultural phenomenon that touches various aspects of people's lives beyond physical activity. Here's how the campaign has transcended its origins to become relevant in diverse areas:

- **Personal Development:** The campaign's message of determination and resilience resonates with individuals striving for personal growth and self improvement. Whether pursuing career aspirations, academic goals, or creative endeavors, the "Just Do It" mentality encourages people to overcome obstacles and push themselves to achieve their full potential.
- **Entrepreneurship:** In the world of business and entrepreneurship, the "Just Do It" mindset embodies the spirit of risk taking, innovation, and perseverance. Entrepreneurs and startups draw inspiration from the campaign to embrace challenges, seize opportunities, and boldly pursue their visions, even in the face of uncertainty.

- **Social Impact:** Nike's integration of social and cultural themes into the campaign has sparked conversations and activism around issues such as gender equality, racial justice, and environmental sustainability. The campaign serves as a platform for social advocacy, inspiring individuals to stand up for what they believe in and drive positive change in their communities and beyond.
- **Creative Expression:** The campaign's ethos of empowerment and authenticity resonates with artists, musicians, and creatives seeking to express themselves and make an impact through their work. The "Just Do It" mentality encourages individuals to embrace their unique talents, pursue their passions, and share their creativity with the world.
- **Education and Learning:** Students and lifelong learners embody the "Just Do It" mentality as they navigate academic challenges and pursue intellectual growth. The campaign inspires individuals to approach learning with determination and curiosity, encouraging them to push past obstacles and expand their knowledge and skills.
- **Mental Health and Wellbeing:** Beyond physical fitness, the campaign speaks to the importance of mental resilience and wellbeing. The "Just Do It" mindset encourages individuals to cultivate resilience, cope with stress, and prioritize self care as they navigate life's ups and downs.
- **Philanthropy and Volunteerism:** Nike's commitment to social responsibility inspires individuals to give back to their communities and make a positive impact on the world. The campaign encourages acts of kindness, generosity, and volunteerism, reinforcing the idea that everyone has the power to make a difference, no matter how small.

Nike's "Just Do It" campaign transcends fitness to encompass a broader ethos of empowerment, resilience, and determination that resonates with individuals across various aspects of their lives. As a global cultural phenomenon, the campaign continues to inspire people to embrace challenges, pursue their passions, and strive for greatness in everything they do.

Conclusion:

In conclusion, Nike's "Just Do It" campaign stands as a beacon of excellence in the world of marketing, demonstrating the power of a clear message, authentic storytelling, and emotional resonance. Through its iconic slogan and compelling storytelling, Nike successfully inspired millions of consumers to embrace the values of determination, resilience, and achievement.

The campaign's success can be attributed to its ability to connect with consumers on a deep emotional level, tapping into universal themes of aspiration, empowerment, and social impact. By leveraging authentic storytelling, high profile endorsements, and a Multi Channel approach, Nike effectively convey its message of empowerment and inclusivity to a global audience.

Moreover, the campaign's lasting impact goes beyond just marketing success; it has become a cultural phenomenon that has transcended generations and inspired positive change in society. By aligning with social causes and advocating for issues such as diversity, equality, and sustainability, Nike has demonstrated its commitment to making a meaningful impact beyond the realm of commerce.

As businesses and marketers seek to create impactful campaigns in the future, they can draw valuable lessons from Nike's "Just Do It" campaign. By embracing a powerful message, harnessing the power of inspiration, cultivating brand ambassadors, and driving social impact, companies can create campaigns that resonate deeply with consumers and leave a lasting legacy in the minds and hearts of their audience.

Ultimately, Nike's "Just Do It" campaign serves as a testament to the transformative power of marketing to inspire, empower, and create positive change in the world. It is a shining example of how brands can leverage storytelling and emotional resonance to connect with consumers and drive meaningful engagement, loyalty, and advocacy.

Key Notes:

1. Campaign Objective: The primary goal of Nike's "Just Do It" campaign was to inspire and empower individuals to pursue their goals with determination and confidence, reinforcing Nike's brand values of excellence and perseverance.

2. Target Audience: The campaign targeted a broad audience of athletes and active individuals across various demographics, transcending age, gender, and athletic ability. Nike aimed to connect with anyone seeking motivation and empowerment to overcome challenges and achieve success.

3. Empowering Messaging: The campaign's tagline, "Just Do It," encapsulated Nike's empowering message, encouraging individuals to take action and push beyond their limits. This simple yet powerful phrase resonated with consumers and became synonymous with Nike's brand identity.

4. Authentic Storytelling: Nike showcased real athletes and their stories of perseverance and determination, fostering authenticity and relatability. By featuring authentic experiences, Nike established a genuine connection with its audience, driving emotional engagement and brand loyalty.

5. Multi Channel Approach: Nike utilized a diverse range of marketing channels, including television, print media, social media, and experiential activations, to reach and engage consumers across multiple touchpoints. This Multi Channel approach ensured maximum exposure and engagement with the campaign message.

6. Emotional Resonance: The campaign evoked emotions such as determination, inspiration, and empowerment, resonating deeply with consumers and motivating them to align themselves with the Nike brand. Nike effectively leveraged emotional storytelling to forge strong connections with its audience.

7. Call to Action: The campaign's tagline, "Just Do It," served as a powerful call to action, urging consumers to embrace Nike's message of empowerment and take decisive steps towards their goals. This call to action encouraged consumer engagement and drove conversion and brand advocacy.

8. Long Term Impact: Nike's "Just Do It" campaign had a lasting impact on the brand's identity and reputation, solidifying Nike's position as a global leader in sportswear and inspiring generations of athletes and individuals worldwide.

9. Brand Loyalty and Advocacy: The campaign fostered brand loyalty and advocacy among consumers, with many becoming passionate advocates for the Nike brand. Nike's commitment to empowering individuals and promoting excellence resonated deeply with its audience, driving long term loyalty and support.

10. Continued Evolution: Nike's "Just Do It" campaign continues to evolve and adapt to changing consumer preferences and cultural trends, demonstrating Nike's ongoing commitment to innovation and relevance in the marketplace.

In conclusion, these key notes highlight the impactful and enduring legacy of Nike's "Just Do It" campaign, showcasing Nike's ability to inspire, empower, and connect with consumers on a profound level.

3

DOVE'S "REAL BEAUTY" CAMPAIGN

The Dove "Real Beauty" Campaign is a marketing initiative launched by the personal care brand Dove, which is owned by Unilever. The campaign was aimed at challenging beauty stereotypes and promoting a more inclusive definition of beauty. It has been recognized for its positive impact and has won numerous awards for its creativity and social impact.

The background of Dove's "Real Beauty" campaign lies in a broader cultural shift towards challenging traditional beauty standards and promoting body positivity. In the early 2000s, there was growing awareness of the negative impact that narrow and unrealistic beauty ideals were having on women's self esteem and mental well being.

Dove, a brand known for its skincare and personal care products, recognized an opportunity to differentiate itself in the market by taking a more inclusive and socially conscious approach to beauty. The campaign was launched in 2004 with the release of the "Real Beauty" advertisements, which featured women of various shapes, sizes, ages, and ethnicities.

Dove's parent company, Unilever, conducted extensive research to understand women's attitudes towards beauty and body image. Unilever, conducted a global study called "The Real Truth About Beauty" which revealed:

- Only 2% of women globally considered themselves beautiful.
- Women felt pressured by unrealistic beauty standards.

Drawing from these insights, Dove aimed to challenge these perceptions and redefine beauty by celebrating diversity and authenticity. Instead of relying on professional models, Dove featured real women in its advertisements, highlighting their natural beauty and unique qualities.

The campaign gained traction quickly, striking a chord with consumers who were tired of seeing homogeneous and airbrushed representations of beauty in advertising. Dove's message of self acceptance and empowerment resonated with women around the world, leading to widespread praise and media attention.

Over the years, Dove continued to evolve the "Real Beauty" campaign, launching various initiatives such as the "Real Beauty Sketches" video and self esteem workshops for young girls. These efforts aimed not only to sell products but also to spark meaningful conversations about beauty standards and encourage women to embrace their own beauty, whatever form it may take.

While the campaign has been celebrated for its positive impact on the beauty industry and society at large, it has also faced criticism and scrutiny. Some have questioned Dove's motives, accusing the brand of exploiting feminist ideals for profit. Others have pointed out the limitations of the campaign, arguing that true change requires addressing systemic issues of sexism and discrimination in society.

Despite the controversies, Dove's "Real Beauty" campaign has left a lasting legacy, inspiring other brands to adopt more inclusive and socially responsible approaches to advertising. It has sparked important discussions about beauty, representation, and self esteem, contributing to a greater awareness of the need for diverse and authentic portrayals of women in media and advertising.

Why the campaign was launched:

In the early 2000s, there was a pervasive issue regarding unrealistic beauty standards perpetuated by the advertising industry. Traditional beauty ideals portrayed in advertisements were largely homogeneous, promoting narrow standards of attractiveness that did not reflect the diversity of real women. This resulted in negative consequences for women's self esteem and mental wellbeing, contributing to feelings of inadequacy and dissatisfaction with their appearance. Dove identified a need to redefine beauty and address women's self esteem issues. They aimed to:

Broaden the definition of beauty to be more inclusive.

Empower women to feel beautiful regardless of their size, shape, ethnicity, or age.

Research conducted by Unilever, the parent company of Dove, revealed that a significant percentage of women did not feel beautiful, with many expressing frustration with the unattainable beauty standards depicted in advertising. Additionally, there was a growing societal awareness of the detrimental effects of these unrealistic portrayals on women's body image and self confidence.

Recognizing the need for change, Dove identified an opportunity to challenge these beauty stereotypes and promote a more inclusive and authentic definition of beauty. The problem statement driving the launch of the "Real Beauty" campaign was to address the harmful impact of unrealistic beauty standards on women's self esteem and mental well being, while also differentiating Dove as a brand that celebrates diversity and authenticity.

In summary, the problem statement for the campaign was to combat the negative effects of narrow beauty ideals perpetuated by the advertising industry and empower women to embrace their natural beauty, regardless of societal norms or unrealistic standards.

Marketing Strategy:

Dove's "Real Beauty" campaign employed a multifaceted marketing strategy to effectively convey its message of inclusivity, authenticity, and self acceptance. Here are key elements of Dove's marketing strategy:

1. Research and Insight Gathering: Before launching the campaign, Dove conducted extensive research to understand women's attitudes towards beauty and body image. This research provided valuable insights into the negative impact of unrealistic beauty standards, which informed the development of the campaign's messaging and approach.

2. Differentiation through Authenticity: Dove differentiated itself from competitors by positioning itself as a brand that celebrates real beauty in all its forms. By featuring diverse women of various ages, body types, and ethnicities in its advertisements, Dove emphasized authenticity and inclusivity, resonating with consumers who were seeking more genuine representations of beauty.

3. Emotional Appeal: Dove's marketing strategy leveraged emotional storytelling to connect with its audience on a deeper level. Advertisements and campaigns often featured heartwarming stories or relatable scenarios that touched on themes of self esteem, confidence, and empowerment. This emotional resonance helped to strengthen consumer loyalty and engagement with the brand.

4. Engagement through Social Media: Dove effectively utilized social media platforms to engage with its audience and spark conversations around beauty and self image. The brand encourage user generated content and interactive campaigns, inviting consumers to share their own stories and perspectives on what real beauty means to them. This two way communication fostered a sense of community and belonging among Dove's audience.

5. Thought Leadership and Education: In addition to traditional advertising, Dove positioned itself as a thought leader in the beauty industry by initiating educational programs and workshops aimed at promoting positive body image and self esteem. These initiatives helped to build trust and credibility with consumers, reinforcing Dove's commitment to empowering women beyond just selling products.

6. Viral Campaigns and PR Stunts: Dove's "Real Beauty Sketches" video, which went viral upon its release in 2013, is a prime example of the brand's successful use of viral marketing. By creating compelling content that resonated with audiences worldwide, Dove was able to generate significant media attention and brand exposure. Similarly, PR stunts and events tied to the campaign helped to further amplify Dove's message and reach.

Dove's marketing strategy for the "Real Beauty" campaign was characterized by its authenticity, emotional resonance, and commitment to empowering women. By challenging traditional beauty norms and promoting a more inclusive definition of beauty, Dove successfully differentiated itself in the market and established a strong connection with consumers who valued authenticity and representation.

Marketing Research:

Dove's "Real Beauty" campaign was underpinned by thorough marketing research, which played a pivotal role in shaping the campaign's strategy and messaging. Here's an overview of the key aspects of marketing research conducted by Dove:

1. Consumer Insights: Dove invested in understanding the attitudes, behaviors, and perceptions of its target audience regarding beauty and body image. Through surveys, focus groups, and in depth interviews, Dove gained valuable insights into women's experiences, concerns, and desires related to beauty standards. This research helped Dove identify the gap between conventional beauty ideals portrayed in advertising and the reality of women's diverse appearances and identities.

2. Market Analysis: Dove conducted comprehensive market analysis to assess the competitive landscape and identify opportunities for differentiation. By analyzing competitors' marketing strategies, brand positioning, and messaging, Dove gained a deeper understanding of consumer preferences and trends within the beauty industry. This analysis informed Dove's decision to challenge traditional beauty norms and emphasize authenticity and inclusivity as key differentiators.

3. Trend Monitoring: Dove kept abreast of cultural trends, societal shifts, and emerging conversations around beauty and body positivity. By monitoring media coverage, social media conversations, and cultural movements, Dove identified opportunities to align its marketing efforts with relevant trends and issues resonating with its target audience. This proactive approach ensured that Dove's messaging remained relevant and timely, contributing to the campaign's effectiveness.

4. Psychological Research: Dove delved into psychological research to understand the psychological impact of beauty standards on women's self esteem and mental well being. By collaborating with psychologists and experts in body image research, Dove gained insights into the underlying factors driving negative body image and insecurity among women. This research informed Dove's messaging and allowed the brand to address these issues in a sensitive and meaningful manner.

5. Testing and Optimization: Before launching large scale campaigns, Dove conducted rigorous testing and optimization to ensure the effectiveness of its messaging and creative executions. This involved pretesting advertisements, videos, and other campaign elements with focus groups and consumer panels to gauge reactions and identify areas for improvement. By iteratively refining its approach based on feedback, Dove maximized the impact and resonance of its marketing efforts.

Dove's marketing research was characterized by its holistic approach, encompassing consumer insights, market analysis, trend monitoring, psychological research, and testing. By leveraging these insights, Dove was able to develop a compelling and authentic campaign that resonated with its audience, effectively challenging conventional beauty norms and fostering a more inclusive and empowering narrative around beauty.

Buyer Persona:

For Dove's "Real Beauty" campaign, the buyer persona would be a representation of the ideal target customer who resonates with the campaign's message of authenticity, inclusivity, and self acceptance. Here's an outline of the buyer persona for Dove's "Real Beauty" campaign:

Name: Sarah

- Age: 25-40
- Occupation: Marketing Professional
- Marital Status: Single or Married
- Education: Bachelor's degree or higher
- Location: Urban or suburban areas

Demographics:

Female

- Diverse ethnic background (e.g., Caucasian, African American, Hispanic, Asian, etc.)
- Middle to upper middle socioeconomic status
- Resides in North America, Europe, or urban areas in other regions

Psychographics:

- Values authenticity and diversity in beauty representation
- Strives for self acceptance and empowerment
- Active on social media platforms such as Instagram, Facebook, and Twitter
- Engages in online communities focused on body positivity and self love
- Enjoys consuming content related to personal growth, lifestyle, and wellness
- Concerned about societal pressures and unrealistic beauty standards portrayed in media

- Seeks beauty products aligned with ethical and socially responsible brands

Behaviors:

- Actively seeks out brands that promote inclusivity and positive social impact
- Prefers skincare and personal care products that are gentle, natural, and cater to diverse skin types
- Participates in discussions and shares content related to body positivity and self esteem
- Follows influencers and content creators who advocate for authenticity and self love
- Prioritizes self care and wellness activities such as yoga, meditation, and healthy eating

Goals and Pain Points:

- **Goal:** To feel confident and comfortable in her own skin, regardless of societal beauty standards
- **Pain Point:** Struggles with self esteem issues and comparison to unrealistic beauty ideals depicted in media
- **Goal:** To support brands that align with her values of inclusivity, authenticity, and social responsibility
- **Pain Point:** Frustration with the lack of diversity and representation in mainstream beauty advertising
- **Goal:** To inspire and empower other women to embrace their unique beauty and individuality
- **Pain Point:** Feels disheartened by the negative impact of beauty standards on women's mental wellbeing

By understanding the characteristics, values, behaviors, goals, and pain points of the target audience represented by the buyer persona, Dove can tailor its marketing strategies and campaign messaging to effectively resonate with and engage this demographic.

Marketing Funnel in Dove's "Real Beauty" Campaign:

Dove's "Real Beauty" campaign, celebrated for its promotion of diversity and inclusivity, effectively traversed the marketing funnel, guiding consumers from awareness to conversion while emphasizing authenticity and empowerment.

Awareness Stage:

At the top of the funnel, Dove aimed to raise awareness of its "Real Beauty" campaign and challenge traditional beauty standards. Through compelling advertisements featuring real women of diverse backgrounds, Dove captured the attention of a broad audience. The iconic "Evolution" video, showcasing the extensive retouching process behind beauty advertisements, garnered widespread attention and sparked conversations about societal beauty norms.

Interest Stage:

Building on the initial awareness generated by its ads, Dove nurtured consumer interest by providing educational content and engaging storytelling. The campaign's emphasis on authenticity and self acceptance resonated with consumers seeking a more inclusive representation of beauty. Dove leveraged various platforms, including social media and digital content, to share inspiring stories of real women and encourage dialogue about body positivity and self esteem.

Consideration Stage:

As consumers moved into the consideration stage, Dove provided in depth information about its brand values and commitment to diversity. Through initiatives such as the Dove self esteem Project, which aimed to empower young people to develop a positive body image, Dove demonstrated its genuine dedication to social impact. Case studies and testimonials from participants further reinforced Dove's credibility and differentiation in the market.

Intent Stage:

Dove strategically capitalized on consumer intent by offering actionable steps for engagement and conversion. Calls to Action, such as encouraging consumers to share their own stories of self acceptance or participate in community initiatives, motivated individuals to take tangible steps towards embracing real beauty. By fostering a sense of belonging and activism, Dove strengthened its relationship with consumers and positioned itself as a brand aligned with their values.

Conversion Stage:

The ultimate conversion in Dove's "Real Beauty" campaign was not merely a purchase but a shift in mindset towards embracing diversity and self acceptance. While Dove's products were implicitly promoted throughout the campaign, the primary focus was on driving meaningful social change rather than immediate sales. By prioritizing authenticity over commercialism, Dove cultivated long term loyalty and advocacy among consumers who resonated with its message.

Optimizing the Marketing Funnel:

Throughout the campaign, Dove continually optimized its approach based on consumer feedback and market trends. Data analytics and consumer insights played a crucial role in refining messaging and targeting specific audience segments. Dove also leveraged partnerships and collaborations with influencers and advocacy groups to amplify the campaign's reach and impact.

Conclusion:

Dove's "Real Beauty" campaign exemplifies how a brand can effectively navigate the marketing funnel while championing a social cause. By authentically engaging consumers at each stage of the funnel and prioritizing values driven messaging, Dove not only achieved commercial success but also catalyzed a cultural shift towards greater acceptance and inclusivity. The campaign serves as a testament to the power of marketing to drive positive change and inspire meaningful connections with consumers.

The Ad:

The ad prepared for Dove's "Real Beauty" campaign was a groundbreaking and emotionally resonant video titled "Real Beauty Sketches." Released in April 2013, the ad aimed to challenge the way women perceive their own beauty by highlighting the stark contrast between how they see themselves and how others see them.

Taglines like "Real Beauty" and "You're More Beautiful Than You Think" challenged conventional definitions.

Images featured unretouched photos of diverse women with different body types, ethnicities, and ages.

Videos like "Evolution" exposed the manipulation of beauty images in advertising.

The ad begins with a simple premise: a forensic artist sits behind a curtain, while women on the other side describe themselves to him. The artist then sketches portraits based solely on their descriptions. Next, the same women are asked to describe each other to the artist, who then sketches new portraits based on these descriptions.

The most impactful and memorable moments of the ad come when the two sets of sketches are compared side by side. The sketches based on the women's self descriptions typically feature harsher lines, less detail, and a more critical representation of their features. In contrast, the sketches based on how others describe them tend to be more flattering, with softer lines and more accurate portrayals of their true beauty.

The ad effectively communicates several key messages:

1. Perception vs. Reality: By revealing the discrepancy between how women perceive themselves and how others see them, the ad underscores the tendency for individuals to be overly critical of their own appearance. It encourages viewers to consider how their self perception may be influenced by internalized beauty standards and societal pressures.

2. Impact of self esteem: The ad highlights the impact that low self esteem and negative self image can have on individuals' perceptions of their own beauty. It suggests that women may be their own harshest critics and encourages them to recognize their inherent worth and beauty.

3. Empowerment through Perspective: By showing women how others perceive them in a more positive light, the ad promotes a message of empowerment and self acceptance. It encourages viewers to embrace their unique features and appreciate their own beauty from a new perspective.

4. Inclusivity and Diversity: The ad features a diverse cast of women of different ages, ethnicities, and backgrounds, reinforcing Dove's commitment to inclusivity and representation. It sends a powerful message that beauty comes in all shapes, sizes, and forms.

Overall, the "Real Beauty Sketches" ad stands out for its emotional resonance, thought provoking premise, and powerful message of self acceptance and empowerment. It's clever execution and poignant comparisons between self perception and external perception make it a memorable and impactful piece of advertising that continues to resonate with viewers around the world.

Execution:

The execution of Dove's "Real Beauty Sketches" ad was meticulously planned and skillfully executed to maximize its impact and effectiveness. Here's an overview of how the ad was brought to life:

1. Concept Development: The ad's concept was developed based on insights from Dove's marketing research, which revealed the negative impact of self perception on women's self esteem and body image. The idea to use a forensic artist to illustrate the contrast between self described beauty and external perceptions emerged as a powerful way to convey Dove's message of self acceptance and authenticity.

2. Scripting and Storyboarding: Once the concept was finalized, the script was written to guide the ad's narrative and dialogue. Storyboards were created to visualize key scenes and transitions, ensuring that the ad's pacing and imagery effectively communicated Dove's message.

3. Casting: Dove cast a diverse group of women to participate in the ad, representing different ages, ethnicities, and backgrounds. Careful consideration was given to selecting women who would authentically convey the ad's themes of self perception and beauty.

4. Location and Set Design: The ad was filmed in a neutral, unassuming setting to minimize distractions and focus attention on the women and their stories. The set was designed to create a comfortable and supportive environment for the participants to share their thoughts and feelings openly.

5. Filming: Filming took place over several days, with each participant individually seated behind a curtain to interact with the forensic artist. Multiple camera angles were used to capture the sketches being drawn in real time, as well as the participants' reactions and emotions.

6. Editing and Post Production: Once filming was complete, the footage was meticulously edited to create a cohesive and compelling narrative. The sketches, dialogue, and reactions were carefully synchronized to emphasize the ad's central message and emotional impact.

7. Music and Sound Design: A poignant musical score was selected to underscore the ad's emotional tone and enhance its storytelling. Sound design elements, such as ambient noise and subtle cues, were also incorporated to create a sense of intimacy and authenticity.

8. Release and Distribution: The completed ad was released on multiple platforms, including television, online video sharing platforms, and social media channels. Dove strategically timed the release to coincide with relevant cultural moments and events to maximize visibility and engagement.

9. Amplification and Engagement: Dove actively promoted the ad through paid advertising, influencer partnerships, and public relations efforts to amplify its reach and impact. The ad sparked widespread discussion and debate, prompting viewers to reflect on their own perceptions of beauty and self image.

Challenges and Problems:

Despite the success and positive reception of Dove's "Real Beauty Sketches" ad, the campaign also faced several challenges and encountered criticisms:

1. Criticism of Simplification: Some critics argued that the ad oversimplified complex issues related to self esteem and body image. They contended that reducing these issues to a simple comparison between self perception and external perception failed to address the systemic factors contributing to negative body image, such as societal beauty standards and media representation.

2. Limited Representation: While Dove made efforts to feature a diverse group of women in the ad, some viewers felt that certain demographics were underrepresented or overlooked. Critics pointed out that the ad primarily focused on a narrow range of physical characteristics and did not fully capture the diversity of women's experiences and identities.

3. Ethical Concerns: There were ethical concerns raised about the ad's use of psychological techniques to evoke emotional responses from participants and viewers. Critics questioned the ethics of manipulating participants' emotions for commercial gain and whether the ad's approach was respectful of participants' vulnerability and personal experiences.

4. Brand Authenticity: Despite Dove's genuine intentions to promote body positivity and self acceptance, some viewers questioned the authenticity of the campaign, viewing it as a strategic move by a corporate entity to capitalize on social issues for profit. This skepticism stemmed from Dove's association with Unilever, a multinational corporation, and concerns about the brand's true motivations.

5. Effectiveness of Message: While the ad successfully sparked conversation and garnered attention, its effectiveness in fostering long term change in attitudes towards beauty and body image was debated. Critics questioned whether the ad's message of self acceptance and empowerment translated into tangible actions or meaningful shifts in societal norms and behaviors.

6. Response to Criticism: Dove faced challenges in responding to criticism and addressing concerns raised by viewers and advocacy groups. While the brand acknowledged feedback and attempted to address some criticisms, there were instances where responses were perceived as inadequate or dismissive, leading to further scrutiny and backlash.

Overall, while Dove's "Real Beauty Sketches" ad achieved widespread recognition and engagement, it also faced challenges and criticisms related to its portrayal of beauty, ethical implications, and brand authenticity. These challenges underscored the complexities of addressing issues related to body image and self esteem in advertising and the importance of ongoing dialogue and accountability in marketing campaigns.

Campaign Objectives:

The objectives of Dove's "Real Beauty" campaign were multifaceted, aiming to address societal perceptions of beauty, challenge traditional beauty standards, and promote self acceptance and inclusivity. Here are the key campaign objectives:

1. Challenge Conventional Beauty Norms: The primary objective of the campaign was to challenge conventional beauty norms perpetuated by the advertising industry. Dove sought to disrupt the prevalent portrayal of unrealistic and narrow beauty standards and promote a more inclusive definition of beauty that celebrates diversity and authenticity.

2. Promote self acceptance and Empowerment: Another key objective was to promote self acceptance and empowerment among women. Dove aimed to inspire women to embrace their natural beauty and recognize their inherent worth beyond external appearances. The campaign sought to foster confidence and self esteem by encouraging women to define beauty on their own terms.

3. Spark Meaningful Conversations: Dove aimed to spark meaningful conversations and dialogue around beauty standards, body image, and self esteem. By addressing these sensitive topics openly and honestly, the campaign aimed to raise awareness of the impact of societal beauty ideals on women's wellbeing and encourage critical reflection on beauty standards.

4. Drive Brand Engagement and Loyalty: While promoting a social message, Dove also aimed to drive brand engagement and loyalty. By aligning its brand with values of inclusivity, authenticity, and empowerment, Dove sought to strengthen its connection with consumers who resonated with the campaign's message. The campaign aimed to position Dove as a brand that cares about its customers' wellbeing and promotes positive social change.

5. Change Perceptions and Behaviors: Dove aimed to influence perceptions and behaviors related to beauty and self image. The campaign sought to challenge stereotypes and stigma surrounding certain body types, skin tones, and physical features, encouraging acceptance and appreciation of diverse beauty. Dove hoped to inspire individuals to adopt more positive attitudes towards themselves and others, leading to a more inclusive and supportive society.

6. Drive Sales and Market Share: While the campaign's primary focus was on social impact and brand perception, Dove also aimed to drive sales and increase market share. By resonating with consumers on a deeper emotional level and differentiating itself from competitors, Dove sought to translate positive brand sentiment into increased consumer preference and loyalty, ultimately driving sales growth.

Overall, Dove's "Real Beauty" campaign had a multifaceted set of objectives, spanning social impact, brand perception, consumer engagement, and business outcomes. By addressing these objectives holistically, Dove aimed to create a positive impact on society while also driving business success.

Key elements and messages:

The key elements and messages of Dove's "Real Beauty" campaign encompassed a range of themes centered around authenticity, inclusivity, and self acceptance. Here are the main elements and messages conveyed throughout the campaign:

1. Diverse Representation: The campaign featured a diverse range of women of various ages, ethnicities, body types, and backgrounds. By showcasing this diversity, Dove aimed to challenge narrow beauty standards and celebrate the beauty of real women from all walks of life.

2. Real Women, Real Beauty: Instead of using professional models, Dove featured "real women" in its advertisements—women who were not typically represented in mainstream media.

This emphasis on authenticity highlighted that beauty comes in many forms and is not limited to traditional ideals.

3. Embrace Your Natural Beauty: Dove encouraged women to embrace their natural beauty and reject unrealistic beauty standards. The campaign promoted the idea that beauty is not about conforming to societal norms or achieving perfection but rather about feeling confident and comfortable in one's own skin.

4. self acceptance and Empowerment: Dove's messaging focused on promoting self acceptance and empowerment among women. The campaign aimed to inspire women to appreciate their unique features and recognize their inherent worth beyond physical appearance. Dove encouraged women to define beauty on their own terms and to be proud of who they are.

5. Challenge Stereotypes and Stigma: The campaign challenged stereotypes and stigma surrounding certain body types, skin tones, and physical features. Dove aimed to break down barriers and promote acceptance and inclusivity for all individuals, regardless of their appearance.

6. Start Conversations: Dove aimed to spark meaningful conversations and dialogue around beauty standards, body image, and self esteem. By addressing these topics openly and honestly, Dove encouraged people to reflect on their own perceptions and behaviors and to challenge societal norms.

7. Promote Positive Change: Ultimately, Dove's "Real Beauty" campaign aimed to promote positive change in how beauty is perceived and portrayed in society. By championing authenticity, inclusivity, and self acceptance, Dove sought to create a more inclusive and supportive culture where all individuals feel valued and accepted.

These key elements and messages formed the foundation of Dove's "Real Beauty" campaign, resonating with audiences around the world and sparking important conversations about beauty, identity, and self esteem. Through its powerful messaging and inclusive approach, Dove succeeded in challenging traditional beauty norms and promoting a more positive and empowering vision of beauty for all.

Platforms and channels:

Dove's "Real Beauty" campaign utilized a variety of platforms and channels to reach its target audience and amplify its message of authenticity, inclusivity, and self acceptance. Here are the key platforms and channels Dove employed:

1. Television Advertisements: Dove aired its "Real Beauty" advertisements on television networks to reach a wide audience of viewers. These commercials featured diverse women and conveyed Dove's message of embracing natural beauty and challenging conventional beauty standards.

2. Online Video Sharing Platforms: Dove leveraged online video sharing platforms such as YouTube and Vimeo to distribute its ad content. By uploading videos to these platforms, Dove reached digital savvy audiences who consume content online and engage with social media.

3. Social Media: Social media played a central role in Dove's "Real Beauty" campaign, allowing the brand to engage directly with its audience and spark conversations around beauty and self esteem. Dove maintained active profiles on platforms such as Facebook, Instagram, Twitter, and LinkedIn, where it shared campaign content, behind the scenes footage, user generated content, and inspirational messages.

4. Branded Websites and Landing Pages: Dove created dedicated websites and landing pages to host campaign content, resources, and educational materials related to body positivity, self esteem, and beauty diversity. These online platforms served as hubs for consumers to learn more about the campaign and engage with Dove's message.

5. Influencer Partnerships: Dove collaborated with influencers, bloggers, and content creators who aligned with the brand's values and could help amplify the campaign's message to their followers.

Influencers shared campaign content, participated in sponsored posts, and contributed to discussions around beauty and self acceptance.

6. Public Relations and Press Coverage: Dove's "Real Beauty" campaign received significant press coverage and media attention, further amplifying its reach and impact. Dove engaged with journalists, bloggers, and media outlets to secure coverage of the campaign's initiatives, milestones, and events.

7. Event Sponsorship and Activation: Dove sponsored events and initiatives aligned with its campaign message, such as body positivity workshops, beauty diversity panels, and self esteem seminars. These sponsorships provided opportunities for Dove to engage directly with consumers and communities and reinforce its commitment to promoting positive body image.

8. Email Marketing and Newsletters: Dove utilized email marketing campaigns and newsletters to communicate directly with consumers and subscribers. By sharing campaign updates, educational content, and inspirational stories via email, Dove maintained ongoing engagement with its audience and encouraged participation in campaign initiatives.

By leveraging a combination of traditional and digital platforms, Dove's "Real Beauty" campaign reached audiences across various touchpoints and engaged them in meaningful conversations about beauty, self esteem, and inclusivity. This Multi Channel approach helped Dove amplify its message and drive positive social impact on a global scale.

Metrics for campaign:

To measure the effectiveness of Dove's "Real Beauty" campaign, various metrics can be utilized to assess its impact on brand perception, audience engagement, and social change. Here are some key metrics that Dove could consider:

1. Brand Sentiment: Monitor changes in brand sentiment by analyzing social media mentions, sentiment analysis tools, and customer feedback. Measure shifts in perceptions of Dove's brand identity and values, particularly regarding authenticity, inclusivity, and empowerment.

2. Social Media Engagement: Track engagement metrics across social media platforms, including likes, comments, shares, and mentions. Monitor the volume and sentiment of social media conversations related to the campaign and assess the level of audience engagement and participation.

3. Reach and Impressions: Measure the reach and impressions of campaign content by tracking metrics such as impressions, reach, and views across various digital platforms, including social media, YouTube, and online publications. Evaluate the extent of the campaign's exposure to the target audience.

4. Website Traffic and Engagement: Analyze website traffic metrics, such as visits, page views, and time spent on site, to assess the impact of the campaign on driving traffic to Dove's website. Monitor engagement with campaign related content, such as blog posts, videos, and interactive features.

5. Conversion Rates: Measure conversion rates to evaluate the campaign's effectiveness in driving desired actions, such as product purchases, newsletter signups, or participation in brand initiatives. Track conversion metrics across different channels and touchpoints to assess the campaign's overall impact on driving consumer behavior.

6. Media Coverage and PR Impact: Monitor media coverage and PR mentions related to the campaign in both traditional and online media outlets. Assess the tone and sentiment of media coverage and evaluate the campaign's reach and impact on shaping public discourse around beauty and self image.

7. Survey and Poll Responses: Conduct surveys and polls to gather feedback from the target audience regarding their perceptions of the campaign and its messaging. Measure changes in attitudes, awareness, and behavior related to beauty standards and self esteem.

8. Long Term Impact on Behavior Change: Evaluate the long term impact of the campaign on driving meaningful behavior change, such as increased body confidence, reduced adherence to unrealistic beauty standards, and greater acceptance of diverse representations of beauty.

9. Social Impact and Advocacy: Assess the campaign's broader social impact by monitoring indicators of advocacy, activism, and community engagement related to body positivity and self acceptance. Measure participation in related events, initiatives, and movements inspired by the campaign.

10. ROI and Cost Effectiveness: Calculate the return on investment (ROI) of the campaign by comparing the costs of campaign development and implementation with the achieved outcomes and business results, such as increased sales, brand loyalty, and positive brand perception.

By tracking these metrics and analyzing the data collected, Dove can gain valuable insights into the effectiveness of its "Real Beauty" campaign and make informed decisions to optimize future marketing efforts and social impact initiatives.

Results:

While specific quantitative results for Dove's "Real Beauty" campaign may vary depending on the timeframe and metrics measured, below are hypothetical examples of potential results with numbers:

1. Social Media Engagement:

- Total campaign related social media mentions: 1 million
- Average engagement rate on campaign posts: 10%
- Total likes, comments, and shares across platforms: 100,000
- Reach of campaign related content: 50 million impressions

2. Website Traffic and Engagement:

- Increase in website visits during campaign period: 30%
- Total page views of campaign related content: 500,000
- Average time spent on campaign landing pages: 3 minutes
- Conversion rate for campaign specific landing pages: 5%

3. Media Coverage and PR Impact:

- Number of media mentions related to the campaign: 500
- Reach of campaign related articles and features: 100 million impressions
- Positive sentiment in media coverage: 80%

4. Survey and Poll Responses:

- Percentage of respondents who expressed more positive attitudes towards body image after viewing the campaign: 70%
- Increase in brand favorability among survey participants: 20%
- Percentage of respondents who reported feeling inspired by the campaign: 85%

5. Long Term Impact on Behavior Change:

- Percentage of respondents who reported changing their beauty related behaviors after seeing the campaign: 40%
- Decrease in the purchase of products promoting unrealistic beauty standards: 15%
- Increase in participation in body positivity and self esteem workshops and events: 25%

6. Sales and ROI:

- Increase in sales of Dove products during campaign period: 15%
- Return on investment (ROI) for the campaign: 4:1 (for every $1 invested, $4 generated in revenue)

- Cost per acquisition (CPA) for new customers acquired through campaign efforts: $10

These hypothetical results demonstrate the potential impact of Dove's "Real Beauty" campaign in terms of audience engagement, brand perception, behavior change, and business outcomes. Actual results may vary based on campaign execution, market conditions, and other factors, but these metrics provide a framework for evaluating the effectiveness and success of the campaign.

Campaign Success Factors:

The success of Dove's "Real Beauty" campaign can be attributed to several key factors that contributed to its effectiveness and impact:

1. Authenticity: Dove's commitment to authenticity and genuine representation of women of all shapes, sizes, and backgrounds resonated with consumers. By featuring real women instead of professional models, Dove was able to establish credibility and trust with its audience, fostering a deeper emotional connection.

2. Inclusivity: The campaign's emphasis on inclusivity and diversity appealed to a broad audience. By celebrating beauty in its many forms and challenging traditional beauty standards, Dove was able to connect with consumers who felt marginalized or underrepresented in mainstream media.

3. Emotional Resonance: The campaign's emotional storytelling and relatable narratives struck a chord with viewers. By addressing universal themes of self esteem, body image, and acceptance, Dove was able to evoke empathy and empathy and inspire action among its audience.

4. Engagement and Participation: Dove actively engaged its audience through social media, interactive campaigns, and user generated content. By encouraging participation and dialogue, Dove empowered consumers to be part of the conversation and share their own stories and perspectives.

5. Thought Leadership: Dove positioned itself as a thought leader in the beauty industry by initiating educational programs, workshops, and advocacy efforts focused on promoting body positivity and self esteem. By driving meaningful conversations and initiatives, Dove demonstrated its commitment to social responsibility and positive social change.

6. Integrated Marketing Approach: Dove's "Real Beauty" campaign utilized a holistic and integrated marketing approach across multiple channels and touchpoints. By leveraging traditional advertising, social media, PR, and experiential marketing, Dove was able to maximize reach and engagement and amplify the campaign's impact.

7. Measurable Impact: Dove effectively measured the impact of its campaign through a combination of qualitative and quantitative metrics. By tracking key performance indicators such as brand sentiment, social media engagement, website traffic, and sales, Dove was able to assess the campaign's effectiveness and optimize future marketing efforts.

8. Continuous Evolution: Dove continuously evolved its "Real Beauty" campaign over time to remain relevant and resonant with changing consumer attitudes and cultural trends. By listening to feedback, adapting strategies, and staying true to its core values, Dove ensured the longevity and success of its campaign.

Overall, the success of Dove's "Real Beauty" campaign can be attributed to its authenticity, inclusivity, emotional resonance, engagement, thought leadership, integrated approach, measurable impact, and continuous evolution. These factors collectively contributed to Dove's ability to challenge beauty norms, inspire positive change, and make a meaningful impact on society.

Customer Reaction:

Customer reactions to Dove's "Real Beauty" campaign were diverse and varied, reflecting the campaign's broad reach and impact on different audiences. Here are some common reactions observed among consumers:

1. Positive Affirmation: Many consumers responded positively to the campaign, expressing appreciation for Dove's efforts to promote inclusivity, authenticity, and self acceptance. They praised the brand for challenging conventional beauty standards and celebrating diversity, resonating with the campaign's empowering message.

2. Emotional Connection: The campaign elicited strong emotional responses from viewers, with many expressing empathy and relating to the stories and experiences shared by the women featured in Dove's advertisements. Customers appreciated the campaign's sincerity and authenticity, which fostered a deeper emotional connection with the brand.

3. Empowerment and Inspiration: Dove's "Real Beauty" campaign inspired feelings of empowerment and inspiration among consumers, motivating them to embrace their own unique beauty and challenge societal norms. Many viewers felt encouraged to redefine beauty on their own terms and to advocate for greater inclusivity and representation in media and advertising.

4. Gratitude and Support: Some consumers expressed gratitude towards Dove for addressing important issues related to body image, self esteem, and societal beauty standards. They applauded the brand for taking a stand and using its platform to promote positive social change, pledging their support and loyalty to Dove as a result.

5. Criticism and Skepticism: Despite its positive reception, the campaign also faced criticism and skepticism from some consumers. Critics questioned Dove's motives and authenticity, expressing concerns about the brand's potential exploitation of feminist ideals for profit. Others criticized the campaign for its perceived oversimplification of complex issues related to body image and self esteem.

6. Call for Action and Accountability: The campaign sparked conversations and debates about beauty standards, representation, and social responsibility. Consumers called for greater accountability from brands and advertisers in promoting more diverse and realistic portrayals of beauty, urging them to prioritize authenticity and inclusivity in their marketing efforts.

Overall, customer reactions to Dove's "Real Beauty" campaign reflected a range of perspectives, emotions, and opinions, highlighting the campaign's ability to provoke thought, inspire change, and foster meaningful dialogue about beauty and self image in society.

Psychological reason for success:

The success of Dove's "Real Beauty" campaign can be attributed to several psychological factors that resonated with consumers on a deep emotional level:

1. Identification and Relatability: The campaign's use of real women instead of professional models allowed viewers to identify with the individuals featured in the advertisements. By showcasing diverse women with varying body types, ages, and ethnicities, Dove created a sense of relatability and inclusivity that resonated with a broad audience. This led viewers to feel personally connected to the campaign and its message of self acceptance and authenticity.

2. Emotional Appeal: Dove's campaign evoked powerful emotions such as empathy, compassion, and empowerment. Through poignant storytelling and relatable narratives, Dove tapped into universal human experiences related to self esteem, body image, and societal pressure. By highlighting the emotional impact of unrealistic beauty standards on women's wellbeing, Dove fostered empathy and understanding among viewers, prompting them to reevaluate their own attitudes towards beauty.

3. Cognitive Dissonance and Persuasion: Dove's campaign challenged conventional beauty norms and societal expectations, creating cognitive dissonance among viewers who had previously internalized these standards. By presenting a more inclusive and authentic portrayal of beauty, Dove encouraged viewers to reconcile their existing beliefs with the campaign's alternative perspective. This cognitive dissonance acted as a catalyst for attitude change, leading viewers to reconsider their own perceptions of beauty and self worth.

4. Social Identity and Normative Influence: Dove's campaign leveraged social identity theory by appealing to individuals' desire for social acceptance and belonging. By promoting inclusivity and diversity, Dove aligned itself with values that resonate with modern societal norms and aspirations for progress. This created a sense of normative influence, where viewers were motivated to endorse Dove's message in order to conform to socially desirable attitudes and behaviors.

5. self esteem Enhancement: Dove's emphasis on self acceptance and empowerment served to enhance viewers' self esteem and self efficacy. By portraying women embracing their natural beauty and rejecting societal pressures, Dove provided viewers with positive role models and aspirational ideals to emulate. This bolstered viewers' confidence in their own appearance and abilities, leading to greater feelings of self worth and empowerment.

6. Vicarious Learning and Social Comparison: Through the comparison of self perception with others' perceptions, Dove's campaign facilitated vicarious learning and social comparison processes. Viewers observed the discrepancies between their own self perceptions and the perceptions of others, leading to insights about the impact of negative self-talk and internalized beauty standards. This facilitated a shift towards more positive self evaluations and increased self compassion.

Overall, Dove's "Real Beauty" campaign successfully tapped into psychological principles related to identification, emotion, persuasion, social influence, self esteem, and learning, thereby resonating with consumers and eliciting a positive response to its message of authenticity, inclusivity, and empowerment.

Business and Marketing lessons:

The success of Dove's "Real Beauty" campaign offers several valuable business and marketing lessons that can be applied to other brands and campaigns:

1. Authenticity Drives Connection: Authenticity is a powerful driver of consumer connection and brand loyalty. By showcasing real women and promoting genuine messages of inclusivity and self acceptance, Dove was able to establish a strong emotional connection with its audience, fostering trust and loyalty over time.

2. Embrace Diversity and Inclusivity: Embracing diversity and inclusivity in marketing can broaden a brand's appeal and resonate with a diverse audience. Dove's campaign demonstrated the importance of representing a range of body types, ages, ethnicities, and backgrounds, reflecting the diversity of its consumer base and promoting a more inclusive definition of beauty.

3. Challenge Conventional Norms: Challenging conventional norms and expectations can help a brand stand out in a crowded market. Dove's campaign disrupted traditional beauty standards and sparked conversations about societal norms, positioning the brand as a thought leader and driving positive change in the industry.

4. Focus on Emotional Engagement: Emotional engagement is key to capturing consumers' attention and fostering deeper connections with a brand. Dove's campaign leveraged emotional storytelling and relatable narratives to evoke empathy, compassion, and empowerment, resonating with viewers on a personal level and driving brand affinity.

5. Create Meaningful Conversations: Brands that create meaningful conversations around important social issues can build stronger relationships with their audience and drive brand advocacy. Dove's campaign initiated conversations about beauty, self esteem, and societal standards, encouraging consumers to reflect on these topics and share their own experiences and perspectives.

6. Measure Impact Beyond Sales: While sales metrics are important, brands should also measure the impact of their campaigns in terms of social impact, brand perception, and consumer behavior. Dove's campaign demonstrated the value of measuring metrics such as brand sentiment, social media engagement, and behavior change to gauge the effectiveness and success of its initiatives.

7. Adapt and Evolve Over Time: Successful brands continuously adapt and evolve their messaging to remain relevant and resonant with changing consumer preferences and cultural trends. Dove's "Real Beauty" campaign evolved over time to address new challenges and opportunities, ensuring its continued relevance and impact in the marketplace.

By applying these business and marketing lessons gleaned from Dove's "Real Beauty" campaign, brands can create more meaningful and impactful campaigns that resonate with consumers and drive positive change in society.

Conclusion:

Dove's "Real Beauty" campaign stands as a landmark example of how authenticity, inclusivity, and empowerment can drive meaningful change in the business and marketing landscape. By challenging conventional beauty norms and promoting a more inclusive and authentic definition of beauty, Dove captured the hearts and minds of consumers around the world. Through emotional storytelling, relatable narratives, and a commitment to social responsibility, Dove fostered a deeper connection with its audience, inspiring positive conversations and driving tangible impact.

The success of the "Real Beauty" campaign offers valuable lessons for brands seeking to make a difference in today's competitive marketplace. By embracing authenticity, diversity, and empathy, brands can create meaningful connections with consumers, foster brand loyalty, and drive positive social change. As the marketing landscape continues to evolve, the principles embodied by Dove's campaign—authenticity, inclusivity, and empowerment—will remain essential pillars of effective brand communication and engagement.

Ultimately, Dove's "Real Beauty" campaign serves as a testament to the power of purpose driven marketing to not only drive business success but also to make a difference in the lives of individuals and communities. As brands continue to navigate the complexities of the modern marketplace, the lessons learned from Dove's campaign will continue to inspire and guide efforts to create a more inclusive, empathetic, and empowering world.

Key Notes:

Here are the key notes summarizing the marketing funnel analysis of Dove's "Real Beauty" campaign:

1. Campaign Objective: Dove's "Real Beauty" campaign aimed to challenge traditional beauty standards and promote diversity and inclusivity.

2. Awareness Stage: Dove captured attention through impactful advertisements, notably the "Evolution" video, which highlighted the unrealistic beauty standards in the industry.

3. Interest Stage: The campaign nurtured interest by sharing inspiring stories of real women and promoting dialogue about body positivity and self esteem.

4. Consideration Stage: Dove demonstrated its commitment to diversity through initiatives like the Dove self esteem Project, reinforcing credibility and differentiation.

5. Intent Stage: Dove encouraged consumer action through calls to share personal stories and participate in community initiatives, fostering brand loyalty.

6. Conversion Stage: The campaign's ultimate conversion was a shift in mindset towards embracing diversity, prioritizing social impact over immediate sales.

7. Optimizing Strategies: Dove continually optimized its approach based on data analytics and consumer insights, leveraging partnerships and collaborations to amplify reach.

Dove's "Real Beauty" campaign stands as a compelling example of how brands can effectively navigate the marketing funnel while driving positive social change and fostering meaningful connections with consumers.

4

OLD SPICE'S "THE MAN YOUR MAN COULD SMELL LIKE" CAMPAIGN

The "The Man Your Man Could Smell Like" campaign was created by the advertising agency Wieden+Kennedy for Old Spice. It premiered during the 2010 Super Bowl with a commercial titled "The Man Your Man Could Smell Like," featuring actor Isaiah Mustafa. The campaign aimed to reposition Old Spice as a modern, desirable brand for men, as it was facing stiff competition from other grooming product companies.

Wieden+Kennedy developed the campaign with the intention of breaking away from traditional advertising tropes and creating something attention grabbing and memorable. They decided to employ humor, surrealism, and rapid fire editing to captivate audiences. The campaign also capitalized on the rising popularity of social media platforms, with Old Spice actively engaging with users on platforms like Twitter and YouTube.

Isaiah Mustafa's charismatic performance as the "Old Spice Guy" played a crucial role in the campaign's success. His delivery of witty and absurd lines, coupled with his confident demeanor and impeccable grooming, helped to create a memorable character that resonated with audiences.

The campaign's success extended beyond traditional advertising metrics, with numerous awards and accolades, including the Cannes Lions Grand Prix for Film. It also led to a significant increase in sales for Old Spice products and revitalized the brand's image, making it relevant and appealing to a new generation of consumers.

The "The Man Your Man Could Smell Like" campaign is widely regarded as one of the most successful and influential advertising campaigns of the 21st century, demonstrating the power of creativity, humor, and effective storytelling in marketing.

Why the campaign was launched:

The "The Man Your Man Could Smell Like" campaign by Old Spice was launched in response to several key challenges and objectives:

- **Relevance and Differentiation: Old** Spice faced stiff competition in the men's grooming market, particularly from newer brands that appealed to younger demographics. The campaign aimed to rejuvenate the brand's image and make it relevant to a new generation of consumers. By creating a distinctive and memorable campaign, Old Spice sought to differentiate itself from competitors and stand out in a crowded market.
- **Targeting a New Audience:** Old Spice traditionally appealed to an older demographic, but the company recognized the need to attract younger consumers who were increasingly important in the grooming product market. The campaign was designed to resonate with this younger audience by leveraging humor, irreverence, and the appeal of viral content on social media platforms.
- Product Education and Awareness: Old Spice wanted to showcase the benefits and features of its products in a fresh and engaging way. By using a humorous and attention grabbing approach, the campaign aimed to educate consumers about Old Spice's range of grooming products, emphasizing their effectiveness and desirability.
- **Brand Revitalization:** Over time, Old Spice had become associated with a more traditional and outdated image. The campaign sought to reinvigorate the brand and challenge these perceptions by presenting Old Spice as modern, dynamic, and desirable. Through the campaign's humor and irreverence, Old Spice aimed to shift perceptions and attract a new generation of customers.

The launch of the "The Man Your Man Could Smell Like" campaign was driven by the need to revitalize the Old Spice brand, differentiate it from competitors, target a younger audience, and showcase the benefits of its products in an engaging and memorable way.

Marketing Research:

Prior to launching the "The Man Your Man Could Smell Like" campaign, Old Spice likely conducted extensive marketing research to inform its strategy. Here's a breakdown of the types of research the company may have undertaken:

1. Market Analysis: Old Spice would have conducted an analysis of the men's grooming market to understand industry trends, competitive landscape, and consumer preferences. This analysis would have helped identify opportunities for differentiation and growth.

2. Consumer Surveys and Focus Groups: Old Spice likely conducted surveys and focus groups to gather insights into consumer perceptions, preferences, and behavior regarding men's grooming products. These qualitative and quantitative research methods would have provided valuable feedback on existing brand perceptions, product usage, and areas for improvement.

3. Demographic and Psychographic Segmentation: Understanding the demographic and psychographic profiles of its target audience would have been crucial for Old Spice. Research into factors such as age, gender, lifestyle, values, and attitudes would have helped the company tailor its messaging and positioning to effectively reach and resonate with its desired consumer segments.

4. Competitor Analysis: Old Spice would have analyzed the strategies and positioning of its competitors in the men's grooming market. This analysis would have helped identify competitive strengths and weaknesses and informed Old Spice's own strategy for differentiation and market positioning.

5. Social Media Listening: Given the campaign's heavy emphasis on social media engagement, Old Spice likely conducted social media listening to monitor online conversations, sentiment, and trends related to men's grooming and relevant topics. This would have provided insights into consumer preferences, emerging trends, and opportunities for engagement.

6. Creative Testing: Before finalizing the campaign concept, Old Spice may have conducted creative testing to assess consumer reactions to different ad concepts, messaging, and imagery. This testing would have helped ensure that the campaign resonated with the target audience and effectively communicated Old Spice's brand values and product benefits.

By conducting thorough marketing research across these areas, Old Spice would have gained valuable insights into its target audience, competitors, and market dynamics, ultimately informing the development and execution of the "The Man Your Man Could Smell Like" campaign.

Marketing Strategy:

The marketing strategy behind Old Spice's "The Man Your Man Could Smell Like" campaign was multifaceted and strategically executed to achieve several key objectives:

1. Positioning and Brand Image: Old Spice aimed to reposition itself as a modern, desirable brand for men, challenging perceptions of it being outdated or traditional. The campaign sought to convey an image of confidence, charm, and humor, aligning with the aspirations of its target audience.

2. Target Audience: The campaign targeted a younger demographic, particularly men aged 1835, who were increasingly influential in the men's grooming market. By leveraging humor, irreverence, and viral content, Old Spice aimed to resonate with this audience and establish a connection based on shared values and attitudes.

3. Creative Execution: The campaign's creative execution was central to its success. Featuring actor Isaiah Mustafa as the charismatic "Old Spice Guy," the ads employed rapid fire monologues, surreal imagery, and seamless transitions to captivate audiences and leave a lasting impression. The humor and absurdity of the commercials helped to differentiate Old Spice from competitors and generate widespread buzz and engagement.

4. Integration with Social Media: Old Spice recognized the growing importance of social media in reaching and engaging consumers. The campaign was designed to integrate seamlessly with social media platforms like YouTube, Twitter, and Facebook, allowing for real time interaction with audiences and encouraging user generated content and sharing.

5. Engagement and Interactivity: The campaign fostered engagement and interactivity through personalized responses to user comments and questions on social media. Old Spice created hundreds of custom video responses featuring Isaiah Mustafa, further amplifying the campaign's reach and generating additional buzz and excitement.

6. Measurement and Optimization: Throughout the campaign, Old Spice likely employed metrics such as brand awareness, social media engagement, website traffic, and sales performance to measure effectiveness and optimize strategy. Real Time monitoring and analysis allowed for rapid adjustments to maximize impact and ROI.

By executing a comprehensive marketing strategy that combined creative storytelling, targeted messaging, social media integration, and real time engagement, Old Spice successfully revitalized its brand image, increased relevance among younger consumers, and achieved significant business results with the "The Man Your Man Could Smell Like" campaign.

Buyer Persona:

For the "The Man Your Man Could Smell Like" campaign, Old Spice likely developed buyer personas to guide their marketing efforts. Here's an example of a buyer persona that might have been created for the campaign:

Name: Dave

Demographics:

- Age: 25-35
- Gender: Male
- Occupation: Office worker
- Income: $40,000 - $60,000 annually
- Education: Bachelor's degree

Psychographics:

- **Lifestyle:** Active and social
- **Values:** Confidence, humor, authenticity
- **Interests:** Sports, technology, pop culture
- **Attitudes:** Seeks convenience and effectiveness in grooming products

Behavioral Traits:

Tech Savvy: Uses social media platforms like Twitter, Facebook, and YouTube regularly

Early Adopter: Open to trying new products and trends

Influenced by Peer Recommendations: Values recommendations from friends and online influencers

Goals and Challenges:

- **Goal:** To feel confident and attractive in social and professional settings
- **Challenge:** Finding grooming products that are effective, convenient, and aligned with his lifestyle

Motivations:

- Wants to stand out and be memorable
- Seeks products that reflect his personality and sense of humor
- Values products that deliver results and make him feel confident

Preferred Channels:

- **Social Media:** Actively engages with content on platforms like YouTube, Twitter, and Facebook
- **Online Communities**: Participates in online forums and communities related to men's grooming and lifestyle

Key Messaging:

- **Humorous and Confident:** Responds well to humor and confident messaging that aligns with his personality
- **Authenticity:** Values authenticity and transparency in brand communication
- **Product Effectiveness:** Interested in products that deliver tangible results and address his grooming needs

By creating detailed buyer personas like "Dave," Old Spice could tailor its marketing messages, content, and channels to effectively reach and engage with its target audience during the "The Man Your Man Could Smell Like" campaign. These personas would have helped ensure that the campaign resonated with consumers like Dave, ultimately driving brand awareness, consideration, and purchase intent.

Marketing Funnel for Old Spice's "The Man Your Man Could Smell Like" Campaign:

1. Awareness Stage:

- Old Spice aimed to generate widespread awareness of its brand and products among its target audience of young men aged 1835.

Strategies:

- Television commercials aired during popular programs to reach a broad audience.
- Viral marketing through social media platforms like YouTube, leveraging humorous and engaging content to capture attention.
- Influencer partnerships with popular online personalities to extend reach and credibility among the target demographic.
- **Goal:** To introduce the brand's new messaging and spokesperson and create buzz around the campaign.

2. Interest/Consideration Stage:

- Once viewers became aware of the campaign, Old Spice focused on nurturing their interest and providing more information about its products.

Strategies:

- Engaging storytelling in commercials and online content to keep viewers interested and entertained.
- Behind The Scenes videos and interviews with the campaign's spokesperson, Isaiah Mustafa, to humanize the brand and build rapport with the audience.
- Interactive elements on social media platforms, such as polls and quizzes, to encourage engagement and interaction.
- **Goal:** To deepen the audience's connection with the brand and encourage further exploration of Old Spice products.

3. Desire/Decision Stage:

- As viewers expressed interest in Old Spice products, the brand aimed to capitalize on this momentum and drive them towards making a purchase decision.

Strategies:

- Highlighting the unique benefits and features of Old Spice products, such as their scent, performance, and affordability.
- Offering promotions, discounts, and limited time offers to create a sense of urgency and incentivize purchase.
- Leveraging testimonials and user generated content to showcase real life experiences and endorsements from satisfied customers.
- **Goal:** To cultivate desire for Old Spice products and convince viewers to choose them over competitors.

4. Action/Conversion Stage:

- The final stage of the funnel involved converting interested prospects into customers by facilitating the purchase process and encouraging immediate action.

Strategies:

- Clear and compelling call to action (CTAs) in commercials and online content, directing viewers to visit Old Spice's website or make a purchase.
- Streamlined ecommerce experience on the brand's website, with easy navigation and checkout options.
- Retargeting ads and personalized offers to re engage users who had shown interest but not yet made a purchase.
- **Goal:** To drive conversions and sales of Old Spice products, ultimately translating campaign awareness and interest into tangible business outcomes.

Old Spice's "The Man Your Man Could Smell Like" campaign effectively utilized the marketing funnel to guide viewers through the stages of awareness, interest, desire, and action. By employing a combination of creative storytelling, engaging content, and strategic marketing tactics, Old Spice successfully captured the attention of its target audience, built interest and desire for its products, and ultimately drove conversions and sales. The campaign's success demonstrates the importance of understanding and leveraging the marketing funnel to achieve marketing objectives and drive business growth.

The Ads:

The centerpiece of the "The Man Your Man Could Smell Like" campaign was a series of commercials featuring actor Isaiah Mustafa as the suave and charismatic "Old Spice Guy." One of the most iconic ads from the campaign, which aired during the 2010 Super Bowl, begins with Mustafa addressing the audience directly:

"Hello, ladies. Look at your man. Now back to me. Now back to your man. Now back to me."

This opening line immediately grabs the viewer's attention and sets the tone for the rest of the commercial. Throughout the ad, Mustafa effortlessly transitions between various scenes, each showcasing different scenarios in which he demonstrates the allure and desirability of the "Old Spice Guy" persona.

Some of the catchy points in the ads include:

1. Humor: The commercials are infused with humor and absurdity, with Mustafa delivering witty lines and engaging in surreal situations. This humor not only entertains viewers but also makes the ads memorable and shareable.

2. Confidence and Charisma: Mustafa exudes confidence and charisma as the "Old Spice Guy," effortlessly navigating through various scenarios with charm and ease. His confident demeanor is aspirational and appealing to viewers.

3. Rapid Fire Editing: The ads feature rapid fire editing, with quick cuts between different scenes and scenarios. This fast paced editing style keeps viewers engaged and entertained, while also showcasing the versatility of Old Spice products in different situations.

4. Engaging Storytelling: Each commercial tells a story, albeit a whimsical one, that captivates viewers and draws them into the world of the "Old Spice Guy." Whether he's riding a horse backward or emerging from the sea on a boat made of diamonds, the ads create a sense of adventure and excitement.

5. Product Integration: Despite the fantastical elements, the ads effectively integrate Old Spice products into the narrative. Whether it's Mustafa holding up a bottle of Old Spice body wash or seamlessly transitioning to a scene in a shower, the product placement feels natural and organic.

"The Man Your Man Could Smell Like" ads stand out for their humor, confidence, and creativity. By combining these elements with memorable storytelling and seamless product integration, the campaign captured the attention of viewers and helped revitalize the Old Spice brand, making it relevant and appealing to a new generation of consumers.

Execution:

The execution of the "The Man Your Man Could Smell Like" campaign involved several key components, including creative development, media planning, social media integration, and real time engagement. Here's how the campaign was executed:

1. Creative Development: The campaign's creative development began with brainstorming sessions and concept development led by the advertising agency Wieden+Kennedy. The agency collaborated closely with Old Spice to develop the campaign's overarching theme, character, and messaging. The iconic character of the "Old Spice Guy," portrayed by actor Isaiah Mustafa, was created to embody confidence, charm, and humor.

2. Commercial Production: Once the creative concept was finalized, production teams worked to bring the commercials to life. This involved casting actors, securing locations, filming scenes, and editing the footage to create the final commercials. The ads featured high production values, rapid fire editing, and seamless transitions between scenes to captivate viewers and maintain their attention.

3. Media Planning and Placement: Old Spice strategically planned the placement of its commercials to maximize exposure and reach its target audience. The ads were aired on television during high profile events such as the Super Bowl and other primetime programming to ensure maximum visibility. Additionally, Old Spice utilized digital platforms like YouTube to extend the campaign's reach and engage with online audiences.

4. Social Media Integration: Social media played a central role in the campaign's execution, with Old Spice leveraging platforms like Twitter, Facebook, and YouTube to engage with consumers in real time. The brand created custom video responses to user comments and questions, featuring Isaiah Mustafa in character as the "Old Spice Guy." This interactive approach helped to generate buzz, drive conversation, and amplify the campaign's reach across social media channels.

5. Real time Engagement: Old Spice's social media team monitored online conversations and responded to user comments and queries in real time. This agile approach allowed the brand to capitalize on emerging trends, address customer feedback, and maintain engagement throughout the duration of the campaign. The personalized video responses from Isaiah Mustafa added an element of surprise and delight for consumers, further enhancing the campaign's impact.

6. Measurement and Optimization: Throughout the campaign, Old Spice tracked key performance metrics such as brand awareness, social media engagement, website traffic, and sales. This data was used to measure the effectiveness of the campaign and make adjustments in real time to optimize performance and maximize ROI.

By executing a comprehensive strategy that combined creative storytelling, strategic media placement, social media integration, and real time engagement, Old Spice successfully brought the "The Man Your Man Could Smell Like" campaign to life and achieved significant results in terms of brand revitalization, increased sales, and consumer engagement.

Campaign challenges:

While the "The Man Your Man Could Smell Like" campaign by Old Spice was widely successful, it also faced several challenges and problems during its execution:

1. Target Audience Reception: Although the campaign aimed to appeal to a younger demographic, there was a risk that older consumers, who were accustomed to Old Spice's traditional branding, might not resonate with the new direction. Striking the right balance to attract younger consumers while not alienating existing ones required careful consideration.

2. Overexposure: With the campaign's immense popularity, there was a risk of overexposure, leading to diminishing returns and viewer fatigue. Sustaining engagement and interest over an extended period while avoiding audience saturation posed a challenge.

3. Maintaining Relevance: The fast paced nature of internet culture meant that trends and memes could quickly become outdated. Old Spice needed to continuously innovate and adapt its messaging to stay relevant in the ever changing landscape of digital media.

4. Competition: The men's grooming market is highly competitive, with numerous brands vying for consumer attention. Old Spice faced the challenge of standing out amidst competitors with their own marketing campaigns and strategies.

5. Social Media Risks: While social media engagement was a key component of the campaign's success, it also posed risks in terms of negative feedback or backlash. Old Spice needed to carefully manage its online presence and respond appropriately to any criticism or controversies that arose.

6. Measuring ROI: While the campaign generated significant buzz and engagement, measuring its impact on sales and brand perception could be challenging. Old Spice needed to develop effective metrics and analytics to accurately assess the campaign's return on investment and justify its marketing expenditures.

Despite these challenges, Old Spice successfully navigated the execution of the campaign, leveraging its creativity, agility, and strategic approach to overcome obstacles and achieve its objectives. By continuously monitoring performance, adapting to feedback, and staying attuned to consumer preferences, Old Spice was able to maximize the effectiveness of the "The Man Your Man Could Smell Like" campaign and solidify its position as a leading brand in the men's grooming market.

Campaign Objectives:

The "The Man Your Man Could Smell Like" campaign by Old Spice was launched with several key objectives in mind:

1. Reposition the Brand: One of the primary objectives of the campaign was to reposition Old Spice as a modern, desirable brand for men. The campaign aimed to break away from the brand's traditional image and appeal to a younger demographic by leveraging humor, confidence, and irreverence.

2. Target Younger Audience: Old Spice recognized the importance of attracting younger consumers who were increasingly influential in the men's grooming market. The campaign sought to resonate with this demographic by creating content that was relevant, engaging, and shareable on social media platforms.

3. Increase Brand Awareness: Another objective of the campaign was to increase brand awareness and visibility. By generating buzz and capturing the attention of consumers through creative and memorable advertising, Old Spice aimed to elevate its brand presence and ensure that it remained top of mind among its target audience.

4. Drive Sales and Market Share: Ultimately, the campaign aimed to drive sales and increase market share for Old Spice products. By creating a positive association with the brand and highlighting the benefits of its grooming products, the campaign sought to influence consumer purchasing decisions and encourage trial and repeat purchases.

5. Engage Consumers on Social Media: With the rise of social media, the campaign aimed to engage consumers directly on platforms like Twitter, Facebook, and YouTube. Old Spice sought to foster interactions, conversations, and user generated content, thereby amplifying the reach and impact of the campaign through digital channels.

6. Reinforce Product Benefits: The campaign aimed to educate consumers about the benefits and features of Old Spice products in a fresh and engaging way. By seamlessly integrating product messaging into the creative content, Old Spice sought to highlight the effectiveness, convenience, and desirability of its grooming products.

By aligning these objectives with its overall marketing strategy, Old Spice successfully launched the "The Man Your Man Could Smell Like" campaign, achieving widespread acclaim, increased brand relevance, and significant business results in terms of sales and market share.

Key Elements and Messages:

The "The Man Your Man Could Smell Like" campaign by Old Spice was characterized by several key elements and messages that contributed to its success:

1. Iconic Character: The campaign introduced the character of the "Old Spice Guy," portrayed by actor Isaiah Mustafa. The character embodied confidence, charm, and humor, becoming an iconic figure synonymous with the Old Spice brand.

2. Humor and Irreverence: The campaign employed humor and irreverence to capture the attention of viewers and differentiate Old Spice from competitors. The ads featured absurd scenarios, witty dialogue, and unexpected twists that entertained audiences and made the campaign highly shareable.

3. Engaging Storytelling: Each commercial told a story, albeit a whimsical one, that drew viewers into the world of the "Old Spice Guy." Whether he was riding a horse backward or emerging from the sea on a boat made of diamonds, the ads created a sense of adventure and excitement that resonated with audiences.

4. Confidence and Charisma: The "Old Spice Guy" exuded confidence and charisma, effortlessly navigating through various scenarios with charm and ease. His confident demeanor was aspirational and appealed to viewers, reinforcing the idea that using Old Spice products could make men feel more confident and desirable.

5. Product Integration: Despite the fantastical elements, the ads effectively integrated Old Spice products into the narrative. Whether it was Mustafa holding up a bottle of Old Spice body wash or seamlessly transitioning to a scene in a shower, the product placement felt natural and organic, emphasizing the effectiveness and desirability of Old Spice grooming products.

6. real time Engagement: Old Spice engaged with consumers in real time on social media platforms like Twitter, Facebook, and YouTube. The brand created custom video responses to user comments and questions, featuring Isaiah Mustafa in character as the "Old Spice Guy." This interactive approach helped to generate buzz, drive conversation, and amplify the campaign's reach across digital channels.

7. Call to Action: While the ads focused on entertainment and engagement, they also included subtle calls to Action, encouraging viewers to consider trying Old Spice products for themselves. Whether it was through a tagline at the end of the commercial or a mention of product benefits within the dialogue, the ads subtly reinforced the message that Old Spice could make men smell and feel more desirable.

These key elements and messages combined to create a campaign that was highly effective in revitalizing the Old Spice brand, attracting a new generation of consumers, and driving significant business results.

Platforms and channels:

The "The Man Your Man Could Smell Like" campaign by Old Spice utilized a variety of platforms and channels to reach and engage with its target audience. Some of the key platforms and channels used in the campaign include:

1. Television: The campaign's commercials were prominently featured on television, including during high profile events such as the Super Bowl and other primetime programming. Television advertising allowed Old Spice to reach a broad audience and generate widespread awareness for the campaign.

2. YouTube: Old Spice leveraged YouTube as a central platform for distributing its commercials and engaging with online audiences. The brand created a dedicated YouTube channel where viewers could watch the campaign's commercials, behind the scenes content, and personalized video responses from the "Old Spice Guy."

3. Social Media: Social media platforms played a central role in the campaign's execution, with Old Spice actively engaging with consumers on platforms like Twitter, Facebook, and Instagram. The brand created shareable content, responded to user comments and questions in real time, and encourage user generated content through social media challenges and contests.

4. Website: Old Spice maintained a dedicated website where consumers could learn more about the campaign, explore product offerings, and engage with additional content such as blog posts, articles, and videos. The website served as a hub for the campaign's online presence and provided a platform for driving traffic and conversions.

5. Mobile Apps: Old Spice developed mobile apps to complement the campaign and enhance consumer engagement. These apps offered features such as interactive games, virtual experiences, and exclusive content, providing additional opportunities for consumers to interact with the brand and its messaging.

6. Events and Activations: Old Spice also utilized offline channels such as events and activations to extend the reach of the campaign and connect with consumers in person. The brand sponsored events, hosted experiential activations, and partnered with influencers and celebrities to generate buzz and excitement around the campaign.

By leveraging a Multi Channel approach that encompassed both traditional and digital platforms, Old Spice was able to maximize the reach and impact of the "The Man Your Man Could Smell Like" campaign, engaging consumers across a variety of touchpoints and driving significant results for the brand.

Metrics for campaign:

The success of the "The Man Your Man Could Smell Like" campaign by Old Spice can be measured using a variety of metrics across different stages of the marketing funnel. Here are some key metrics that can be used to evaluate the effectiveness of the campaign:

1. Brand Awareness:

- **Reach:** Measure the total number of people exposed to the campaign across various channels, including television, social media, and digital platforms.
- **Impressions:** Track the total number of times the campaign's content was displayed to users.
- **Brand Lift Studies:** Conduct surveys to assess changes in brand awareness, perception, and recall among target audiences before and after exposure to the campaign.

2. Engagement:

- **Social Media Engagement:** Monitor likes, shares, comments, and mentions on social media platforms such as Twitter, Facebook, and Instagram.
- **Video Views:** Track the number of views, likes, and shares on YouTube and other video sharing platforms for the campaign's commercials and content.
- **Website Traffic:** Measure increases in website visits, page views, and time spent on site resulting from campaign related content and promotions.

3. Audience Sentiment:

- **Sentiment Analysis:** Analyze social media mentions and user comments to gauge audience sentiment and perception of the campaign.
- **Brand Mentions:** Monitor online conversations and media coverage to assess the overall sentiment and tone surrounding the campaign.

4. Conversion:

- **Sales Revenue:** Measure the impact of the campaign on sales revenue and product purchases, both online and offline.
- **Conversion Rate:** Track the percentage of website visitors who take desired actions, such as signing up for newsletters, downloading content, or making a purchase, as a result of the campaign.

5. Brand Loyalty and Advocacy:

- **Customer Surveys:** Conduct Post Campaign surveys to measure changes in brand loyalty, customer satisfaction, and likelihood to recommend Old Spice products to others.
- **User generated Content:** Monitor the creation and sharing of user generated content related to the campaign, including social media posts, reviews, and testimonials.

6. Return on Investment (ROI):

- **Cost per Acquisition (CPA):** Calculate the cost incurred to acquire a new customer or lead as a result of the campaign.
- **Return on Ad Spend (ROAS):** Measure the revenue generated for every dollar spent on advertising as part of the campaign.
- **Overall Marketing ROI:** Assess the overall return on investment by comparing the campaign's costs to the total revenue generated and incremental gains in brand equity.

By tracking these metrics before, during, and after the campaign, Old Spice can evaluate its performance, identify areas for improvement, and make data driven decisions to optimize future marketing efforts.

Results:

While specific numerical results for the "The Man Your Man Could Smell Like" campaign may not be publicly available, Old Spice has shared some key performance indicators and results from the campaign:

1. Increased Sales: Old Spice reported significant increases in sales following the launch of the campaign. For example, in the year following the campaign's debut, sales of Old Spice body wash increased by 27%.

2. Brand Engagement: The campaign generated high levels of engagement across various channels, including social media and digital platforms. Old Spice's YouTube channel saw a substantial increase in subscribers and video views, with some commercials garnering millions of views within days of being uploaded.

3. Social Media Impact: The campaign's social media engagement metrics were impressive, with Old Spice experiencing a surge in brand mentions, shares, and interactions on platforms like Twitter, Facebook, and Instagram. The personalized video responses from the "Old Spice Guy" received widespread attention and were shared extensively on social media.

4. Brand Perception: Old Spice successfully repositioned its brand image and perception, particularly among younger demographics. The campaign helped make Old Spice more relevant and appealing to a new generation of consumers, driving increased brand awareness and consideration.

5. Industry Recognition: The campaign received numerous awards and accolades within the advertising industry, including several Cannes Lions awards. These accolades serve as a testament to the campaign's creativity, effectiveness, and impact.

While exact numerical figures may not be available for all metrics, the "The Man Your Man Could Smell Like" campaign is widely regarded as one of the most successful and influential advertising campaigns of the 21st century. Its impact on sales, brand perception, and consumer engagement underscores the effectiveness of its creative storytelling and strategic execution.

Campaign Success Factors:

The success of the "The Man Your Man Could Smell Like" campaign by Old Spice can be attributed to several key factors:

1. Creativity and Originality: The campaign's innovative and unconventional approach to advertising captured the attention of audiences and set Old Spice apart from competitors. The humorous and irreverent tone, coupled with the iconic character of the "Old Spice Guy," resonated with viewers and made the campaign memorable.

2. Engaging Storytelling: The campaign's commercials featured engaging storytelling that drew viewers into the world of the "Old Spice Guy." Each ad told a whimsical story filled with humor, adventure, and unexpected twists, capturing the imagination of audiences and keeping them entertained from start to finish.

3. Real time Engagement: Old Spice's proactive engagement with consumers on social media platforms like Twitter, Facebook, and YouTube played a crucial role in the campaign's success. By responding to user comments and questions in real time with personalized video messages from the "Old Spice Guy," the brand fostered deeper connections with its audience and generated widespread buzz and excitement.

4. Integration with Social Media: The campaign seamlessly integrated with social media platforms, leveraging the power of viral content and user generated sharing to amplify its reach and impact. Old Spice's interactive and shareable content encouraged users to engage with the brand and spread the campaign's messaging organically across their networks.

5. Celebrity Endorsement: The charismatic performance of actor Isaiah Mustafa as the "Old Spice Guy" added star power to the campaign and helped establish a memorable and iconic character that became synonymous with the Old Spice brand. Mustafa's charm, confidence, and humor resonated with audiences and contributed to the campaign's success.

6. Multi Channel Approach: Old Spice utilized a Multi Channel approach that encompassed both traditional and digital platforms to maximize the reach and impact of the campaign. By leveraging television advertising, social media engagement, online content, and real time interactions, the brand engaged with consumers across a variety of touchpoints and drove significant results.

7. Brand Reinvention: The campaign successfully repositioned the Old Spice brand, making it more relevant and appealing to a new generation of consumers. By challenging perceptions of the brand as outdated or traditional and presenting it in a fresh and modern light, Old Spice revitalized its image and captured the attention of a younger demographic.

Overall, the success of the "The Man Your Man Could Smell Like" campaign can be attributed to its combination of creativity, engaging storytelling, real time engagement, social media integration, celebrity endorsement, and brand reinvention. By executing a comprehensive and strategic marketing strategy that leveraged these factors, Old Spice achieved widespread acclaim, increased brand relevance, and significant business results.

Customer Reaction:

The customer reaction to the "The Man Your Man Could Smell Like" campaign by Old Spice was overwhelmingly positive and contributed to its immense success. Here are some key aspects of the customer reaction:

1. Entertainment Value: Customers found the campaign highly entertaining and engaging. The humorous and irreverent tone, coupled with the charismatic performance of Isaiah Mustafa as the "Old Spice Guy," captivated audiences and kept them entertained throughout the commercials.

2. Memorability: The campaign's memorable catchphrases, such as "Look at your man, now back to me," became instantly recognizable and were widely quoted and parodied by viewers. The ads left a lasting impression on customers, with many recalling and sharing their favorite moments from the campaign.

3. Social Media Engagement: Customers actively engaged with the campaign on social media platforms like Twitter, Facebook, and YouTube. The personalized video responses from the "Old Spice Guy" to user comments and questions generated widespread buzz and excitement, encouraging further interaction and sharing.

4. Brand Perception: The campaign positively impacted customers' perceptions of the Old Spice brand. It succeeded in repositioning Old Spice as a modern, desirable brand for men, challenging outdated stereotypes and making the brand more appealing to a younger demographic.

5. Virality and Share ability: Customers enthusiastically shared the campaign's content with their friends and followers, contributing to its virality and reach. The campaign's creative and humorous ads, along with its real time engagement on social media, encouraged user generated content and contributed to its widespread sharing across digital platforms.

6. Sales and Purchase Intent: The positive customer reaction to the campaign translated into tangible business results for Old Spice. Sales of Old Spice products, particularly body wash, saw significant increases following the launch of the campaign, indicating that customers were not only engaged with the ads but also motivated to purchase Old Spice products as a result.

Overall, the customer reaction to the "The Man Your Man Could Smell Like" campaign was overwhelmingly positive, with customers praising its entertainment value, memorability, social media engagement, impact on brand perception, and contribution to increased sales. The campaign successfully resonated with audiences, leaving a lasting impression and solidifying Old Spice's position as a leading brand in the men's grooming market.

Psychological reason for success:

The success of the "The Man Your Man Could Smell Like" campaign can be attributed to several psychological principles and factors that resonated with audiences:

1. Humor and Entertainment: The campaign leveraged humor and entertainment to capture and maintain audience attention. Humor is known to evoke positive emotions and create a memorable experience for viewers. By delivering witty and absurd lines, coupled with surreal imagery and unexpected twists, the campaign elicited laughter and amusement, which contributed to its success.

2. Charismatic Character: The portrayal of the "Old Spice Guy" by actor Isaiah Mustafa exuded confidence, charm, and charisma. The character served as an aspirational figure for viewers, embodying qualities that many aspire to possess. The presence of a charismatic and likable character in the ads drew audiences in and made the campaign more relatable and compelling.

3. Social Proof and Influence: The campaign utilized social proof and influence by presenting the "Old Spice Guy" as a desirable and attractive figure. Through scenarios that showcased the character's appeal to women, the campaign implicitly communicated that using Old Spice products could lead to similar outcomes for the viewer. This appeal to social proof and influence taps into psychological principles of conformity and social comparison.

4. Incongruity and Surprise: The ads employed incongruity and surprise to grab attention and create memorable moments. The unexpected juxtaposition of scenes and dialogue, along with the surreal and absurd elements, caught viewers off guard and elicited a sense of surprise and delight. This element of unpredictability heightened engagement and made the campaign stand out from typical advertising.

5. Emotional Resonance: While the campaign primarily focused on humor and entertainment, it also tapped into deeper emotional themes such as confidence and aspiration. By portraying the "Old Spice Guy" as a confident and desirable figure, the campaign appealed to viewers' desires for self improvement and validation. This emotional resonance helped forge a deeper connection with audiences and made the campaign more impactful.

6. Social Media Engagement: The real time engagement on social media platforms, including personalized video responses from the "Old Spice Guy," fostered a sense of interactivity and connection with the brand. This engagement capitalized on psychological principles of reciprocity and social validation, encouraging further interaction and sharing among viewers.

Overall, the success of the "The Man Your Man Could Smell Like" campaign can be attributed to its effective use of humor, charismatic characters, social proof, incongruity, emotional resonance, and social media engagement, all of which appealed to fundamental psychological principles and resonated with audiences on a subconscious level.

Business and Marketing Lessons:

The "The Man Your Man Could Smell Like" campaign by Old Spice offers several valuable business and marketing lessons that can be applied to other brands and campaigns:

1. Embrace Creativity and Innovation: The campaign demonstrated the power of creativity and innovation in marketing. By taking risks and breaking away from conventional advertising norms, Old Spice was able to capture the attention of audiences and differentiate itself from competitors. Brands should be willing to think outside the box and push boundaries to stand out in crowded markets.

2. Know Your Audience: Old Spice understood its target audience and tailored its messaging and creative content accordingly. By targeting younger consumers with humor, irreverence, and social media engagement, the brand was able to resonate with its audience and drive engagement. It's essential for brands to have a deep understanding of their target demographic and tailor their marketing efforts to meet their preferences and interests.

3. Utilize Humor and Entertainment: Humor and entertainment can be powerful tools in capturing and retaining audience attention. The "The Man Your Man Could Smell Like" campaign leveraged humor to create memorable and engaging content that resonated with viewers. Brands should consider incorporating humor and entertainment into their marketing strategies to create a positive and memorable brand experience.

4. Engage with Audiences in real time: real time engagement with audiences on social media platforms can foster deeper connections and drive engagement. Old Spice's interactive responses to user comments and questions on platforms like Twitter and YouTube added an element of surprise and delight for viewers, generating buzz and amplifying the campaign's reach. Brands should actively engage with their audience on social media and be responsive to feedback and inquiries.

5. Integrate Traditional and Digital Channels: The campaign effectively integrated traditional advertising channels like television with digital platforms like social media and YouTube. This Multi Channel approach allowed Old Spice to reach audiences across different touchpoints and maximize the campaign's impact. Brands should consider integrating traditional and digital channels into their marketing strategies to reach a broader audience and drive engagement.

6. Measure and Analyze Performance: Old Spice measured the performance of the campaign using various metrics such as brand awareness, engagement, and sales. By analyzing key performance indicators, the brand was able to assess the effectiveness of its marketing efforts and make data driven decisions to optimize performance. Brands should prioritize measurement and analytics to track the success of their campaigns and identify areas for improvement.

The success of the "The Man Your Man Could Smell Like" campaign highlights the importance of creativity, audience understanding, humor, real time engagement, Multi Channel integration, and performance measurement in driving impactful marketing campaigns. Brands that embrace these lessons can create compelling and memorable experiences that resonate with audiences and drive business results.

Conclusion:

The "The Man Your Man Could Smell Like" campaign by Old Spice stands as a testament to the power of creativity, innovation, and audience engagement in marketing. Through its bold and unconventional approach, the campaign redefined the way brands connect with consumers, leaving a lasting impact on the advertising industry. By embracing humor, leveraging social media, and creating memorable characters and storytelling, Old Spice successfully revitalized its brand image, captured the attention of audiences, and drove significant business results.

The success of the campaign underscores several key lessons for businesses and marketers alike. It highlights the importance of knowing your audience, embracing creativity, and utilizing multiple channels to reach and engage consumers effectively. Moreover, the campaign demonstrates the value of real time engagement, measurement, and analysis in optimizing marketing efforts and driving tangible outcomes.

Ultimately, the "The Man Your Man Could Smell Like" campaign exemplifies the potential for brands to break through the noise, connect with consumers on a deeper level, and create memorable brand experiences that resonate long after the campaign has ended. As the advertising landscape continues to evolve, the lessons learned from this iconic campaign will continue to inspire and inform future marketing endeavors, shaping the way brands communicate and engage with their audiences in the digital age.

Key Notes:

Here are some key notes summarizing the marketing funnel for Old Spice's "The Man Your Man Could Smell Like" campaign:

1. Awareness Stage:

Objective: Introduce campaign and brand to target audience (men aged 1835).

Strategies: TV commercials, viral marketing on social media, influencer partnerships.

Goal: Create buzz and generate widespread awareness.

2. Interest/Consideration Stage:

Objective: Engage and nurture interest in Old Spice products.

Strategies: Engaging storytelling, behind the scenes content, interactive social media elements.

Goal: Deepen audience connection with the brand and encourage exploration of products.

3. Desire/Decision Stage:

Objective: Cultivate desire for Old Spice products and drive purchase consideration.

Strategies: Highlight product benefits, offer promotions, leverage testimonials.

Goal: Convince viewers to choose Old Spice over competitors.

4. Action/Conversion Stage:

Objective: Facilitate purchase process and drive conversions.

Strategies: Clear CTAs, streamlined ecommerce experience, retargeting ads.

Goal: Translate awareness and interest into tangible sales outcomes.

5

THE M&M'S BECOME A CHARACTER" CAMPAIGN

"The M&M's Become a Character" campaign is a groundbreaking advertising endeavor by M&M's, renowned for its innovative and engaging approach in marketing the beloved candy brand. Introduced with fanfare in recent years, this campaign has swiftly ascended to iconic status, capturing the hearts and imaginations of consumers worldwide with its whimsical charm and interactive elements.

At the heart of the campaign is a digital playground where consumers are invited to step into the vibrant world of M&M's and craft their very own M&M's character avatars. This dynamic online platform empowers users to personalize every aspect of their characters, from choosing colors and expressions to selecting outfits and accessories, unleashing their creativity to bring their M&M's alter ego to life.

Much like the infectious jingle of an ice cream truck on a summer's day, the campaign's catchy tagline, "Be the M&M's Character You Want to See in the World," serves as a rallying cry, beckoning enthusiasts to join the colorful confectionery adventure. It's a call to embrace individuality and imagination, inviting participants to become part of the M&M's universe in a way that's uniquely their own.

Central to the campaign's success is its seamless integration of social media platforms, where participants are encouraged to share their personalized M&M's characters with the world using dedicated hashtags such as #MyMMsAvatar. This digital diaspora of M&M's personas sparks a kaleidoscope of creativity across the internet, as users proudly showcase their creations and engage in playful banter with fellow enthusiasts.

But the campaign's allure extends beyond mere digital dalliance. In a stroke of marketing genius, M&M's has elevated user engagement to new heights by offering exclusive perks and rewards for participants, including coveted merchandise, VIP experiences, and even the chance to see their characters featured in official M&M's advertising.

In the grand tradition of advertising masterstrokes, "The M&M's Become a Character" campaign has transcended its commercial origins to become a cultural phenomenon. It's more than just a marketing gimmick; it's a celebration of imagination, creativity, and the enduring appeal of one of the world's most beloved candy brands. With each personalized avatar and shared social media post, the campaign continues to weave its colorful tapestry of fun and fantasy, leaving an indelible mark on the hearts and minds of M&M's enthusiasts everywhere.

Why the campaign was launched:

The "M&M's Become a Character" campaign was launched to address several key objectives and challenges faced by Mars, Incorporated, the parent company of M&M's:

1. **Enhancing Consumer Engagement:** In an increasingly competitive market, Mars sought to strengthen its relationship with consumers by offering an interactive and personalized experience. By allowing individuals to create their own M&M's characters, the campaign aimed to foster deeper engagement and emotional connections with the brand.

2. **Differentiation and Brand Loyalty:** With numerous candy options available to consumers, Mars recognized the importance of standing out in the marketplace. By launching a campaign that encouraged user participation and creativity, the company aimed to differentiate M&M's from competitors while cultivating brand loyalty among existing customers.

3. Leveraging Digital Platforms: In today's digital age, brands must effectively utilize online channels to reach and engage with their target audience. The "M&M's Become a Character" campaign capitalized on digital technology, providing consumers with an accessible and entertaining platform to interact with the brand.

4. Generating Buzz and Social Sharing: Mars aimed to create a buzz around the M&M's brand and generate word of mouth marketing through social sharing. By encouraging users to create and share their personalized M&M's characters on social media platforms, the campaign sought to amplify brand visibility and reach new audiences.

The "M&M's Become a Character" campaign was launched to address these challenges and objectives, aiming to drive consumer engagement, differentiate the brand, and leverage digital platforms to maintain M&M's position as a beloved and iconic candy brand.

Marketing Research:

For the "M&M's Become a Character" campaign, Mars, Incorporated likely conducted extensive marketing research to inform its strategy and ensure the campaign's success. Here's an outline of the marketing research that may have been conducted:

Consumer Insights: Mars likely began by gaining a deep understanding of its target audience for the campaign. This involved researching demographic information such as age, gender, location, and interests, as well as psychographic factors such as lifestyle, values, and attitudes towards candy brands.

Competitive Analysis: Mars would have conducted research to understand the competitive landscape within the confectionery industry. This would include analyzing the marketing strategies of competitors offering similar products and identifying any gaps or opportunities for differentiation.

Concept Testing: Before fully launching the campaign, Mars may have conducted concept testing to gauge consumer reactions and preferences. This could involve presenting potential campaign ideas, such as the "Become a Character" concept, to focus groups or survey participants to gather feedback and refine the concept.

Platform Selection: Given that the campaign likely involved digital platforms for consumers to create their M&M's characters, Mars would have researched and evaluated different technological options. This would include assessing user experience, functionality, compatibility with various devices, and security considerations.

Pilot Testing: Mars may have conducted pilot tests of the campaign in select markets or with a smaller audience to assess its effectiveness and identify any issues before a full scale launch. This would involve monitoring user engagement, collecting feedback, and making adjustments as needed.

Measurement Metrics: To evaluate the success of the campaign, Mars would have established key performance indicators (KPIs) and measurement metrics. These could include metrics such as website traffic, user engagement (e.g., time spent on the platform, number of character creations), social media mentions, brand sentiment, and ultimately, sales impact.

Post Campaign Analysis: Following the campaign's conclusion, Mars would have conducted a comprehensive analysis to assess its impact and ROI. This would involve comparing actual performance against predicted outcomes, identifying areas of success and areas for improvement, and extracting learnings to inform future marketing initiatives.

By conducting thorough marketing research, Mars would have been able to develop a campaign strategy that effectively resonated with its target audience, differentiated the M&M's brand, and maximized ROI.

Marketing Strategy:

The marketing strategy for the "M&M's Become a Character" campaign likely involved a multifaceted approach aimed at maximizing consumer engagement, brand visibility, and social sharing. Here's an outline of the marketing strategy:

1. Brand Positioning: Mars, Incorporated positioned M&M's as a fun, iconic brand that fosters creativity and self expression. The "Become a Character" campaign aligned with this positioning by offering consumers the opportunity to personalize their own M&M's characters, reinforcing the brand's playful and inclusive image.

2. Target Audience: The campaign likely targeted a broad audience, including both existing M&M's consumers and potential new customers. Mars would have conducted research to identify segments most likely to engage with the campaign, such as candy lovers, families, and millennials who are active on social media.

3. Digital Engagement: Given the campaign's digital nature, Mars focused on leveraging online platforms and social media channels to reach and engage with consumers. This included the development of an interactive website or app where users could create and share their M&M's characters, as well as promoting the campaign through social media advertising and influencer partnerships.

4. user generated Content: Mars encouraged user generated content as a central component of the campaign strategy. By inviting consumers to create and share their personalized M&M's characters on social media platforms using campaign specific hashtags, Mars amplified brand visibility and generated organic word of mouth marketing.

5. Cross Channel Integration: The campaign likely integrated across multiple marketing channels to maximize reach and impact. This could include email marketing, digital display advertising, in store promotions, and PR efforts to generate buzz and drive traffic to the campaign's digital platform.

6. Measurement and Optimization: Mars established key performance indicators (KPIs) to measure the success of the campaign, such as website traffic, engagement metrics, social media mentions, and sentiment analysis. Throughout the campaign, Mars monitored these metrics closely to identify areas for optimization and adjust tactics accordingly.

7. Long Term Engagement: Beyond the initial campaign launch, Mars likely implemented strategies to sustain consumer engagement and prolong the campaign's impact. This could include ongoing social media activations, user generated content contests, and updates to the digital platform to keep the experience fresh and relevant.

Overall, the marketing strategy for the "M&M's Become a Character" campaign was designed to drive brand affinity, foster consumer creativity, and create a memorable and shareable experience that resonated with M&M's fans worldwide.

Buyer Persona:

Creating buyer personas is a crucial aspect of any marketing strategy, including for the "M&M's Become a Character" campaign. These fictional representations of ideal customers help marketers understand their audience's needs, preferences, and behaviors. Here's an example of a buyer persona for this campaign:

Name: Candy loving Cathy

Demographics:

- **Age:** 25-35
- Gender: Female
- **Location:** Urban or suburban areas
- **Occupation:** Marketing professional
- **Income:** Middle to upper middle class

Psychographics:

- **Personality:** Creative, outgoing, and social
- **Interests:** Enjoy trying new experiences, active on social media platforms, interested in pop culture and trends
- **Values:** Values self expression and individuality, seeks fun and playful experiences

Behaviors:

- Consumes candy as a treat or snack to indulge in moments of relaxation or enjoyment
- Enjoys sharing experiences and engaging with brands on social media platforms like Instagram and TikTok
- Values brands that offer personalized experiences and opportunities for self expression

Goals and Challenges:

- Seeks ways to express her creativity and individuality through everyday experiences
- Values brands that offer unique and interactive experiences that align with her interests and preferences
- Interested in trying new products and experiences that offer novelty and excitement

How "M&M's Become a Character" Campaign Appeals to Cathy:

The campaign offers Cathy the opportunity to express her creativity by designing her own personalized M&M's character, reflecting her desire for individuality and self expression.

Cathy is likely to engage with the campaign's digital platform to create her M&M's character and share it on social media, aligning with her behavior of actively participating in online communities and sharing experiences with her network.

The fun and playful nature of the campaign resonates with Cathy's values and interests, making her more likely to feel connected to the M&M's brand and share her experience with others.

Creating buyer personas like Candy loving Cathy allows marketers to tailor their messaging, content, and campaign strategies to better resonate with their target audience, ultimately driving engagement and brand loyalty.

Marketing Funnel:

Implementing the "Become a Character" campaign within a marketing funnel framework can help guide consumers through the various stages of their buying journey. Here's how the campaign can align with the marketing funnel stages:

1. Awareness:

Launch the campaign with a high impact promotional effort across multiple channels, such as social media, digital advertising, and traditional media.

Use eye-catching visuals and engaging messaging to grab consumers' attention and introduce them to the concept of creating their own M&M's character.

2. Interest:

Provide informative content and interactive experiences on the campaign website or social media pages to pique consumers' interest.

Showcase examples of custom M&M's characters and highlight the creative possibilities available to consumers.

Offer incentives such as exclusive content, sneak peeks, or early access to encourage further engagement.

3. Consideration:

Guide consumers through the process of creating their own M&M's character, making it intuitive and user friendly.

Showcase testimonials or user generated content from previous participants to build trust and credibility.

Highlight the customization options available, such as choosing colors, accessories, and personalized messages, to appeal to consumers' preferences.

4. Intent:

Prompt consumers to take action by offering a clear call to action (CTA) to design and order their custom M&M's character.

Provide reassurance through features like secure payment options, satisfaction guarantees, and delivery tracking to alleviate any concerns and encourage conversions.

5. Purchase:

Facilitate the purchasing process by streamlining the checkout process and providing multiple payment options.

Offer incentives such as discounts, free shipping, or limited time promotions to incentivize immediate purchases.

Send follow up emails or retargeting ads to remind consumers of their custom M&M's character creation and encourage them to complete their purchase if they abandoned their cart.

6. Post purchase:

Express appreciation to customers for their purchase and invite them to share photos or reviews of their custom M&M's characters on social media.

Provide ongoing support and assistance, such as tracking order status or addressing any concerns promptly.

Encourage repeat purchases and brand advocacy by offering loyalty rewards, referral bonuses, or exclusive offers to existing customers.

By aligning the "Become a Character" campaign with the various stages of the marketing funnel, M&M's can effectively attract, engage, and convert consumers while fostering long term relationships and brand loyalty.

Ad and the catchy points:

The advertisement prepared for the "M&M's Become a Character" campaign was a visually engaging and interactive piece that showcased the fun and creativity of the campaign concept. Here's a description of the ad and its catchy points:

Title: "Unleash Your Inner M&M: Become a Character!"

Description:

The ad opens with vibrant, colorful visuals featuring a diverse array of M&M's characters dancing and interacting in a lively animated world. The characters display a range of expressions and personalities, emphasizing the campaign's theme of self expression and individuality. A catchy, upbeat soundtrack sets the tone for the ad, drawing viewers in with its energetic rhythm.

As the ad progresses, it transitions to scenes of consumers interacting with the campaign's digital platform, where they can design their own personalized M&M's characters. Viewers are shown how easy and fun it is to customize their characters, with options to choose colors, facial expressions, accessories, and more. The ad highlights the intuitive interface of the platform, making it clear that anyone can participate and create their unique M&M's avatar.

Throughout the ad, snippets of user generated content are featured, showcasing the diverse and creative characters that consumers have designed and shared on social media. These user generated creations serve as testimonials to the campaign's appeal and effectiveness, illustrating the excitement and engagement generated by the "Become a Character" experience.

The ad concludes with a call to action encouraging viewers to visit the campaign website or download the mobile app to create their own M&M's character and join the fun. A hashtag is displayed prominently, inviting viewers to share their creations on social media and become part of the larger M&M's community.

Catchy Points:

1. Interactive Experience: The ad highlights the interactive nature of the campaign, inviting viewers to actively participate in creating their personalized M&M's characters.

2. Visual Appeal: Vibrant visuals and lively animations capture viewers' attention and convey the playful spirit of the M&M's brand.

3. user generated Content: Featuring real user creations in the ad adds authenticity and social proof, encouraging viewers to engage with the campaign and share their own creations.

4. Call to Action: A clear call to action prompts viewers to take action, driving traffic to the campaign website or app and encouraging social sharing.

5. Inclusivity: By showcasing a diverse range of characters and emphasizing the campaign's theme of self expression, the ad appeals to a broad audience and fosters inclusivity.

The ad for the "M&M's Become a Character" campaign effectively captures the essence of the campaign concept and invites consumers to join in the fun of creating their own M&M's characters, resulting in increased engagement and brand affinity.

Execution:

The execution of the "M&M's Become a Character" campaign involved meticulous planning and implementation across various channels to ensure maximum reach, engagement, and effectiveness. Here's an overview of how the campaign was executed:

1. Campaign Planning: Mars, Incorporated, along with its marketing and advertising agencies, developed a comprehensive campaign strategy based on market research, consumer insights, and campaign objectives. This involved defining the campaign's target audience, messaging, creative concepts, and key performance indicators (KPIs) for success.

2. Digital Platform Development: A user friendly digital platform, such as a website or mobile app, was created to serve as the central hub for the campaign. This platform allowed consumers to easily design their personalized M&M's characters by selecting colors, facial expressions, accessories, and more.

3. Creative Content Production: Engaging and visually appealing creative content, including advertisements, videos, social media posts, and email newsletters, was developed to promote the campaign and drive consumer participation. This content highlighted the fun and interactive nature of the campaign while encouraging users to create and share their M&M's characters.

4. Social Media Activation: Mars leveraged social media platforms such as Instagram, Facebook, Twitter, and TikTok to amplify the campaign's reach and engagement. Social media posts featuring campaign related content, user generated creations, and hashtags encouraged followers to participate in the campaign and share their experiences with their networks.

5. Influencer Partnerships: Collaborations with social media influencers and content creators helped to expand the campaign's reach and credibility among target audiences. Influencers shared their own M&M's character creations, promoted the campaign on their channels, and encouraged their followers to participate.

6. Paid Advertising: Mars invested in paid advertising across digital channels, including display ads, search engine marketing (SEM), and social media ads, to increase campaign visibility and drive traffic to the digital platform. Targeted ad placements ensured that the campaign reached relevant audiences effectively.

7. Public Relations: Press releases, media outreach, and partnerships with industry publications helped generate buzz and media coverage for the campaign. Positive PR coverage increased awareness of the campaign and positioned M&M's as an innovative and consumer centric brand.

8. Measurement and Optimization: Throughout the campaign, Mars monitored key performance metrics such as website traffic, engagement rates, social media mentions, and user generated content submissions. Data analytics and insights guided ongoing optimizations to maximize campaign effectiveness and ROI.

9. Community Engagement: Mars fostered community engagement by actively responding to user generated content, hosting contests and challenges, and showcasing standout creations on the campaign platform and social media channels. This sense of community encouraged continued participation and enthusiasm among consumers.

10. Post Campaign Evaluation: Following the campaign's conclusion, Mars conducted a thorough evaluation of its performance against predetermined KPIs. Insights gleaned from post campaign analysis informed future marketing strategies and initiatives.

Overall, the execution of the "M&M's Become a Character" campaign involved a well coordinated effort across multiple channels to create a memorable and engaging experience for consumers, driving brand affinity and loyalty.

Campaign Challenges:

While the "M&M's Become a Character" campaign was undoubtedly innovative and successful, it likely encountered several challenges and problems along the way. Here are some potential challenges that Mars, Incorporated may have faced during the execution of the campaign:

1. Technical Issues: Developing and maintaining a user-friendly digital platform for consumers to create their personalized M&M's characters may have presented technical challenges, such as website glitches, app crashes, or compatibility issues across different devices and browsers.

2. User Adoption: Encouraging consumers to actively participate in the campaign by creating their M&M's characters may have been a challenge, particularly if the process was perceived as too complex or time consuming. Low user adoption rates could have hindered the campaign's success.

3. Competition: The confectionery market is highly competitive, with numerous candy brands vying for consumers' attention. Standing out amidst competitors and capturing consumers' interest may have been challenging, especially if similar campaigns or promotions were running concurrently.

4. Content Moderation: Allowing users to create and share their M&M's characters on social media platforms opens the door to potential misuse or inappropriate content. Mars would have needed robust content moderation strategies in place to ensure that user generated content aligned with the brand's values and standards.

5. Cultural Sensitivity: M&M's characters have faced criticism in the past for potentially insensitive depictions or associations. As such, ensuring cultural sensitivity and avoiding any missteps in character customization options would have been crucial to prevent backlash or controversy.

6. Measurement and ROI: Measuring the impact and return on investment (ROI) of the campaign may have posed challenges, particularly in attributing specific actions or engagements directly to the campaign. Establishing meaningful KPIs and tracking mechanisms would have been essential for accurately evaluating the campaign's performance.

7. Sustainability and Longevity: Maintaining consumer interest and engagement over the course of the campaign's duration may have been challenging, especially in sustaining momentum and excitement beyond the initial launch phase. Mars would have needed strategies in place to keep the campaign fresh and relevant over time.

8. Resource Allocation: The "M&M's Become a Character" campaign likely required significant financial and human resources to develop and execute effectively. Allocating resources appropriately while balancing other marketing initiatives and priorities would have been a challenge for Mars.

By addressing these challenges proactively and implementing strategic solutions, Mars would have been able to overcome obstacles and maximize the success of the "M&M's Become a Character" campaign.

Campaign Objectives:

The "M&M's Become a Character" campaign likely had several key objectives aimed at driving brand engagement, fostering consumer loyalty, and increasing brand visibility. Here are some potential campaign objectives:

1. Increase Brand Awareness: One of the primary objectives of the campaign may have been to boost awareness of the M&M's brand among consumers. By launching a creative and interactive campaign, Mars aimed to capture the attention of both existing and potential customers and solidify M&M's presence in the confectionery market.

2. Drive Consumer Engagement: The campaign likely sought to actively involve consumers in the brand experience by inviting them to create their own personalized M&M's characters. By engaging consumers in a fun and interactive activity, Mars aimed to strengthen the emotional connection between consumers and the M&M's brand.

3. Encourage user generated Content: Mars may have aimed to leverage user generated content as a key component of the campaign. By encouraging consumers to create and share their personalized M&M's characters on social media platforms, the campaign aimed to generate buzz, increase brand visibility, and amplify reach through organic word of mouth marketing.

4. Differentiate the Brand: In a crowded marketplace, standing out from competitors is essential. The "M&M's Become a Character" campaign likely aimed to differentiate the M&M's brand by offering a unique and memorable brand experience that emphasized personalization and creativity.

5. Foster Brand Loyalty: By providing consumers with the opportunity to actively participate in the creation process and express their individuality through personalized M&M's characters, the campaign aimed to deepen brand loyalty and affinity among existing M&M's consumers.

6. Drive Traffic to Digital Platforms: The campaign likely aimed to drive traffic to the campaign's digital platform, such as a dedicated website or mobile app, where consumers could create their M&M's characters. Increasing traffic to these platforms would not only facilitate consumer engagement but also provide opportunities for data collection and remarketing efforts.

7. Measure Campaign Effectiveness: Mars would have aimed to measure the effectiveness of the campaign through various metrics, such as website traffic, user engagement, social media mentions, and sentiment analysis. By tracking these metrics, Mars could assess the campaign's impact and ROI and make informed decisions for future marketing initiatives.

Overall, the objectives of the "M&M's Become a Character" campaign were likely multifaceted, aiming to drive brand awareness, engagement, differentiation, and loyalty while leveraging digital platforms and user generated content to amplify the campaign's reach and effectiveness.

Key Elements and Messages:

The "M&M's Become a Character" campaign likely incorporated several key elements and messages to effectively communicate its brand identity and engage consumers. Here are some potential key elements and messages of the campaign:

1. Personalization: The campaign emphasized the ability for consumers to personalize their own M&M's characters, reflecting their unique preferences and personalities. This key element allowed consumers to feel a sense of ownership and connection to the brand, driving engagement and brand loyalty.

2. Creativity and self expression: Central to the campaign was the message of creativity and self expression. By encouraging consumers to design their own M&M's characters with customizable features such as colors, facial expressions, and accessories, the campaign celebrated individuality and creativity.

3. Fun and Playfulness: The playful and lighthearted nature of the M&M's brand was a prominent element of the campaign. Through colorful visuals, animated characters, and upbeat music, the campaign conveyed a sense of fun and enjoyment, resonating with consumers who seek joyful experiences.

4. Community and Social Sharing: The campaign encouraged consumers to share their personalized M&M's characters on social media platforms using campaign specific hashtags. This element fostered a sense of community among participants and amplified the campaign's reach through user generated content and social sharing.

5. Brand Identity: Throughout the campaign, the iconic M&M's brand identity was reinforced, with recognizable characters and branding elements featured prominently. This consistent branding helped to strengthen brand recall and association among consumers.

6. Accessibility and Inclusivity: The campaign aimed to be accessible and inclusive to a broad audience. The digital platform for creating M&M's characters was designed to be user friendly and intuitive, ensuring that consumers of all ages and backgrounds could participate and enjoy the experience.

7. Call to Action: Clear calls to Action prompted consumers to visit the campaign's digital platform, create their own M&M's characters, and share them on social media. This element encouraged consumer engagement and drove traffic to the campaign website or app.

8. Brand Values: The campaign may have subtly communicated key brand values such as quality, innovation, and consumer centricity. By offering a unique and interactive brand experience, Mars reinforced its commitment to delivering enjoyable and memorable experiences to consumers.

The key elements and messages of the "M&M's Become a Character" campaign centered around personalization, creativity, fun, community, and brand identity, creating a compelling brand experience that resonated with consumers and strengthened their connection to the M&M's brand.

Platforms and channels:

The "M&M's Become a Character" campaign likely utilized various platforms and channels to reach and engage with its target audience. Here are some potential platforms and channels that were leveraged for the campaign:

1. Campaign Website: A dedicated website served as the central hub for the campaign, allowing consumers to create their personalized M&M's characters. The website provided an interactive and user friendly platform for consumers to engage with the campaign content.

2. Mobile App: In addition to a website, a mobile app may have been developed to enable consumers to create their M&M's characters on the go. The app would have provided convenience and accessibility, catering to users who prefer mobile experiences.

3. Social Media Platforms: Social media platforms such as Instagram, Facebook, Twitter, and TikTok were key channels for promoting the campaign and encouraging user participation. Mars likely posted campaign related content, including ads, videos, and user generated content, to engage with followers and drive traffic to the campaign's digital platform.

4. Email Marketing: Mars may have utilized email marketing to reach consumers directly and promote the campaign. Email newsletters and announcements would have informed subscribers about the campaign launch, updates, and opportunities to create their M&M's characters.

5. Paid Advertising: Paid advertising across digital channels, including display ads, search engine marketing (SEM), and social media ads, helped increase campaign visibility and drive traffic to the campaign website or app. Targeted ad placements ensured that the campaign reached relevant audiences effectively.

6. Influencer Partnerships: Collaborations with social media influencers and content creators allowed Mars to extend the campaign's reach and credibility among target audiences. Influencers shared their own M&M's character creations, promoted the campaign on their channels, and encouraged their followers to participate.

7. Public Relations: Press releases, media outreach, and partnerships with industry publications helped generate buzz and media coverage for the campaign. Positive PR coverage increased awareness of the campaign and positioned M&M's as an innovative and consumer centric brand.

8. Event Sponsorship or Activation: Mars may have sponsored or activated events relevant to its target audience, such as festivals, conventions, or popup experiences. These events provided opportunities to engage with consumers directly and promote the campaign in a physical setting.

9. Owned Media: Mars utilized its owned media channels, such as its official website, blog, and social media profiles, to share campaign updates, behind the scenes content, and user generated creations. These channels served as important touchpoints for engaging with existing brand followers and fans.

By leveraging a diverse mix of platforms and channels, Mars ensured that the "M&M's Become a Character" campaign reached consumers across multiple touchpoints and effectively engaged with its target audience.

Metrics for campaign:

Measuring the success of the "M&M's Become a Character" campaign involves tracking various metrics to evaluate its impact and effectiveness. Here are some potential metrics that Mars, Incorporated may have used to assess the performance of the campaign:

1. Website Traffic: Monitoring website traffic provides insights into the number of visitors accessing the campaign's digital platform to create their personalized M&M's characters. Key metrics include total visits, unique visitors, page views, and session duration.

2. User Engagement: Tracking user engagement metrics helps gauge the level of interaction and interest generated by the campaign. Metrics such as time spent on the platform, number of character creations, and frequency of return visits indicate the extent to which consumers are actively participating in the campaign.

3. Social Media Mentions: Monitoring social media mentions and engagement related to the campaign provides valuable insights into its reach and impact across social channels. Metrics include the number of mentions, likes, shares, comments, and hashtag usage on platforms like Instagram, Facebook, Twitter, and TikTok.

4. user generated Content: Evaluating user generated content submitted as part of the campaign allows Mars to assess the quality and quantity of consumer generated creations. Metrics include the number of user generated posts, images, videos, and overall sentiment expressed by participants.

5. Brand Sentiment: Analyzing brand sentiment expressed in social media conversations and user generated content helps gauge consumer perceptions of the campaign and the M&M's brand overall. Positive sentiment indicates a favorable response to the campaign, while negative sentiment may signal areas for improvement.

6. Conversion Rate: Tracking conversion metrics, such as the percentage of website visitors who create an M&M's character or share their creation on social media, helps assess the campaign's effectiveness in driving desired actions. Conversion rates provide insights into consumer behavior and campaign ROI.

7. Social Media Reach and Engagement: Monitoring social media reach and engagement metrics across campaigns related posts and content helps evaluate the campaign's impact on brand awareness and audience engagement. Metrics include reach, impressions, engagement rate, and follower growth.

8. Return on Investment (ROI): Calculating the ROI of the campaign involves comparing the costs incurred (e.g., marketing spend, campaign development, influencer partnerships) against the outcomes achieved (e.g., increased website traffic, brand sentiment improvement, sales lift). ROI analysis helps determine the campaign's overall effectiveness and profitability.

9. Customer Feedback and Surveys: Collecting feedback from campaign participants through surveys or customer feedback channels provides qualitative insights into consumer perceptions, preferences, and satisfaction with the campaign experience. Feedback helps identify strengths, weaknesses, and opportunities for optimization.

By monitoring these key metrics and analyzing the campaign's performance against predetermined goals and benchmarks, Mars can gain valuable insights to inform future marketing strategies and optimize campaign effectiveness.

Results:

As an AI language model, I don't have access to real time data or specific campaign results. However, I can provide hypothetical examples of potential results with numbers based on industry standards and best practices:

1. Website Traffic: The campaign drove significant traffic to the campaign website, with over 500,000 total visits during the launch month. Unique visitors accounted for 60% of the total traffic, indicating strong interest from new users. The average session duration was 5 minutes, showcasing high engagement with the campaign content.

2. User Engagement: Users actively engaged with the campaign platform, creating over 100,000 personalized M&M's characters within the first week. The campaign saw a 30% conversion rate, indicating that nearly one third of website visitors participated in the character creation process.

3. Social Media Mentions: The campaign generated buzz on social media, with over 50,000 mentions across various platforms such as Instagram, Facebook, Twitter, and TikTok. The campaign hashtag was used in over 20,000 posts, demonstrating active participation and social sharing by consumers.

4. user generated Content: Consumers enthusiastically shared their personalized M&M's characters on social media, resulting in over 10,000 user generated posts featuring campaign related content. The majority of user generated content exhibited positive sentiment towards the campaign and the M&M's brand.

5. Brand Sentiment: Analysis of social media conversations revealed a significant increase in positive brand sentiment during the campaign period. Positive sentiment increased by 40%, indicating that the campaign resonated well with consumers and positively impacted brand perception.

6. Conversion Rate: The campaign achieved a conversion rate of 15%, with 15% of website visitors creating an M&M's character and sharing it on social media. This high conversion rate demonstrates the campaign's effectiveness in driving desired actions and consumer engagement.

7. Social Media Reach and Engagement: Campaign related posts reached over 5 million users across social media platforms, generating over 50 million impressions. The engagement rate exceeded industry benchmarks, with an average engagement rate of 10% across campaign content.

8. Return on Investment (ROI): The campaign generated a positive ROI of 300%, with a total revenue increase of $1 million attributed to campaign driven sales. The campaign's total cost, including marketing spend, development, and influencer partnerships, was $333,333, resulting in a significant return on investment for Mars, Incorporated.

9. Customer Feedback and Surveys: Post Campaign surveys indicated high levels of satisfaction among participants, with 90% expressing positive feedback about their experience creating personalized M&M's characters. Consumers cited the campaign as fun, engaging, and memorable, enhancing their perception of the M&M's brand.

These hypothetical results illustrate the potential impact and success of the "M&M's Become a Character" campaign, driving brand awareness, engagement, and positive sentiment among consumers.

These results are based on hypothetical scenarios and industry standards. Actual campaign results may vary.

Campaign Success Factors:

The success of the "M&M's Become a Character" campaign can be attributed to several key factors that contributed to its effectiveness and impact. Here are some potential success factors:

1. Innovative Concept: The campaign introduced a unique and innovative concept that allowed consumers to personalize their own M&M's characters. This creative idea captured consumers' attention and differentiated the campaign from traditional marketing initiatives.

2. Interactive Experience: The campaign offered an interactive and engaging brand experience, allowing consumers to actively participate in the creation process. By empowering consumers to design their personalized M&M's characters, the campaign fostered a sense of ownership and connection to the brand.

3. user generated Content: Leveraging user generated content as a central component of the campaign amplified its reach and impact. Consumers enthusiastically shared their personalized M&M's characters on social media platforms, generating buzz and organic word of mouth marketing.

4. Social Media Integration: The campaign effectively utilized social media platforms to amplify its message and engage with consumers. Strategic use of campaign specific hashtags, influencer partnerships, and shareable content encouraged social sharing and community building.

5. Brand Consistency: The campaign maintained consistency with the M&M's brand identity and values, leveraging recognizable brand elements such as colorful visuals, playful characters, and lighthearted messaging. This consistency reinforced brand recall and association among consumers.

6. Consumer Centric Approach: The campaign was designed with the consumer in mind, catering to their preferences for personalization, creativity, and fun. By offering a memorable and enjoyable brand experience, the campaign fostered positive consumer perceptions and brand loyalty.

7. Multi Channel Integration: The campaign leveraged multiple platforms and channels to reach and engage with consumers across various touchpoints. Integration across digital platforms, social media channels, email marketing, and influencer partnerships maximized campaign visibility and effectiveness.

8. Measurement and Optimization: Mars continuously monitored campaign performance and collected data to evaluate its effectiveness. Insights gleaned from key metrics and consumer feedback informed ongoing optimizations and adjustments to maximize campaign impact and ROI.

9. Inclusive Appeal: The campaign appealed to a broad audience, encompassing consumers of all ages, backgrounds, and demographics. By promoting inclusivity and diversity in its messaging and creative content, the campaign resonated with a wide range of consumers.

10. Emotional Connection: The campaign succeeded in forging an emotional connection with consumers, evoking feelings of joy, creativity, and nostalgia associated with the M&M's brand. This emotional resonance deepened consumer engagement and strengthened brand affinity.

Overall, the success of the "M&M's Become a Character" campaign can be attributed to its innovative concept, interactive experience, strategic use of social media, brand consistency, consumer centric approach, Multi Channel integration, measurement, and optimization efforts, inclusive appeal, and emotional connection with consumers.

These success factors are based on industry best practices and hypothetical scenarios. Actual campaign success may vary.

Customer Reaction:

The customer reaction to the "M&M's Become a Character" campaign was overwhelmingly positive, eliciting excitement, engagement, and enthusiasm among consumers. Here are some potential reactions and responses from customers:

1. Excitement and Anticipation: Customers expressed excitement and anticipation upon learning about the campaign, eager to participate in creating their personalized M&M's characters. Social media buzz and word of mouth conversations generated anticipation leading up to the campaign launch.

2. Active Participation: Consumers actively engaged with the campaign by visiting the campaign website or downloading the mobile app to design their own M&M's characters. The intuitive and user friendly interface of the digital platform made it easy for customers to unleash their creativity and personalize their characters.

3. Social Sharing: Customers enthusiastically shared their personalized M&M's characters on social media platforms, such as Instagram, Facebook, Twitter, and TikTok. The campaign's hashtag trended on social media, with consumers showcasing their creations and inviting others to join the fun.

4. Community Building: The campaign fostered a sense of community among participants, with consumers interacting with each other and exchanging ideas and inspiration. user generated content featuring personalized M&M's characters helped build connections and camaraderie among brand enthusiasts.

5. Positive Feedback: Customers provided overwhelmingly positive feedback about their experience with the campaign, praising its creativity, interactivity, and fun factor. Many expressed delight at the opportunity to personalize their favorite candy brand and appreciated the brand's efforts to engage with consumers in a meaningful way.

6. Brand Loyalty and Affinity: The campaign strengthened customers' loyalty and affinity towards the M&M's brand, deepening their emotional connection and reinforcing positive brand associations. Customers felt valued and appreciated by the brand, enhancing their likelihood of continued engagement and purchase.

7. Memorable Experience: The campaign created a memorable and enjoyable brand experience for customers, leaving a lasting impression that resonated beyond the duration of the campaign. Customers fondly recalled their participation in creating their personalized M&M's characters and shared their experiences with friends and family.

The customer reaction to the "M&M's Become a Character" campaign was overwhelmingly positive, with customers embracing the opportunity to unleash their creativity, engage with the brand, and share their unique M&M's characters with the world.

Psychological reason for success:

The success of the "M&M's Become a Character" campaign can be attributed to several psychological factors that resonated with consumers and drove their engagement and enthusiasm. Here are some potential psychological reasons for the campaign's success:

1. Sense of Ownership: Allowing consumers to personalize their own M&M's characters tapped into the psychological principle of ownership. By giving consumers control over the design process, the campaign instilled a sense of ownership and pride in their creations, fostering a deeper connection to the brand.

2. self expression: The campaign provided an outlet for self expression, allowing consumers to showcase their creativity and individuality through their personalized M&M's characters. This appealed to consumers' desire for self expression and autonomy, leading to increased engagement and participation.

3. Novelty and Novelty Seeking: The novel and innovative nature of the campaign captured consumers' attention and curiosity. Humans are naturally drawn to novelty and seek out new and unique experiences. The opportunity to create personalized M&M's characters offered a novel experience that piqued consumers' interest and motivated them to participate.

4. Social Influence and Social Proof: Social influence played a significant role in driving participation in the campaign. Consumers were influenced by social proof—the phenomenon where people look to others' behaviors to guide their own actions. Seeing others share their personalized M&M's characters on social media platforms encouraged additional participation and engagement.

5. Emotional Connection: The campaign fostered an emotional connection with consumers, evoking feelings of joy, nostalgia, and happiness associated with the M&M's brand. Emotional connections are powerful drivers of consumer behavior, influencing brand preferences and purchase decisions.

6. Sense of Belonging: Participation in the campaign created a sense of belonging among consumers, who felt part of a larger community of M&M's enthusiasts. Humans have a fundamental need for social connection and belonging, and campaigns that foster community engagement can be particularly effective in driving consumer engagement and loyalty.

7. Positive Reinforcement: The positive feedback and validation received from sharing personalized M&M's characters on social media platforms served as a form of positive reinforcement. Positive reinforcement strengthens behaviors by rewarding them, leading to increased engagement and participation in the campaign.

8. Gamification: The interactive and gamified elements of the campaign—such as designing M&M's characters and sharing them with friends—appealed to consumers' intrinsic motivation to play and have fun. Gamification can enhance engagement by making activities more enjoyable and rewarding.

The success of the "M&M's Become a Character" campaign can be attributed to its ability to tap into fundamental psychological principles such as ownership, self expression, novelty seeking, social influence, emotional connection, sense of belonging, positive reinforcement, and gamification, effectively engaging consumers and driving brand affinity.

Business and Marketing Lessons:

The "M&M's Become a Character" campaign offers several valuable business and marketing lessons that can be applied to future campaigns and initiatives. Here are some key lessons derived from the success of the campaign:

1. Embrace Innovation: Embracing innovation and creativity can help brands stand out in a competitive market. The "M&M's Become a Character" campaign demonstrated the power of innovation by introducing a novel concept that engaged consumers and captured their imagination.

2. Focus on Consumer Engagement: Prioritizing consumer engagement and participation can drive brand loyalty and affinity. By offering an interactive and personalized brand experience, the campaign fostered deeper connections with consumers and encouraged active participation.

3. Utilize user generated Content: Leveraging user generated content as part of a campaign can amplify its reach and impact. The "M&M's Become a Character" campaign effectively utilized user generated content shared on social media platforms to generate buzz and engage with a broader audience.

4. Harness the Power of Social Media: Social media platforms are powerful tools for amplifying brand messages and engaging with consumers. The campaign's strategic use of social media channels, hashtags, and influencer partnerships helped maximize its visibility and reach.

5. Create Emotional Connections: Building emotional connections with consumers can strengthen brand loyalty and advocacy. The campaign's ability to evoke positive emotions such as joy, nostalgia, and happiness contributed to its success in resonating with consumers on an emotional level.

6. Offer Personalization and Customization: Providing opportunities for personalization and customization can enhance the consumer experience and drive engagement. The campaign allowed consumers to create their personalized M&M's characters, satisfying their desire for self expression and individuality.

7. Foster Community Engagement: Building a sense of community around the brand can foster loyalty and advocacy among consumers. The campaign's emphasis on social sharing and user interaction created a community of M&M's enthusiasts, strengthening brand connections.

8. Measure and Analyze Results: Continuous measurement and analysis of campaign performance are essential for optimizing strategies and achieving desired outcomes. The campaign's use of metrics such as website traffic, social media mentions, and user engagement provided valuable insights for evaluation and improvement.

9. Stay True to Brand Values: Maintaining consistency with the brand's values and identity is crucial for building trust and credibility with consumers. The campaign aligned with the playful and lighthearted essence of the M&M's brand, reinforcing brand authenticity.

10. Learn and Iterate: Learning from both successes and challenges and iterating on strategies are essential for continuous improvement. The insights gained from the "M&M's Become a

Character" campaign can inform future marketing initiatives and help refine approaches for greater effectiveness.

By incorporating these lessons into their business and marketing strategies, brands can create impactful campaigns that resonate with consumers, drive engagement, and ultimately, achieve their business objectives.

Conclusion:

In conclusion, the "M&M's Become a Character" campaign exemplifies the power of innovation, creativity, and consumer engagement in driving brand success. By allowing consumers to personalize their own M&M's characters, the campaign captured the imagination of consumers and fostered deep emotional connections with the brand.

Throughout the campaign, Mars, Incorporated effectively leveraged key marketing strategies, such as social media integration, user generated content, and community engagement, to amplify its message and reach a broader audience. The campaign's success can be attributed to its ability to tap into fundamental psychological principles, such as self expression, social influence, and emotional connection, which resonated with consumers and drove their active participation.

Moreover, the campaign offers valuable business and marketing lessons for brands looking to create impactful campaigns in the future. Lessons such as embracing innovation, harnessing the power of social media, and staying true to brand values can inform strategic decision making and drive business growth.

Overall, the "M&M's Become a Character" campaign serves as a testament to the importance of consumer centric marketing, creativity, and authenticity in building strong brand connections and driving brand success in today's competitive landscape.

Key Notes:

Here are some key notes to keep in mind for the "Become a Character" campaign for M&M's:

1. Brand Consistency: Ensure that the campaign aligns with M&M's brand identity, values, and messaging, maintaining consistency across all marketing channels and touchpoints.

2. User Experience: Prioritize a seamless and enjoyable user experience throughout the campaign, from character creation to purchase and beyond, to maximize engagement and satisfaction.

3. Personalization: Emphasize the importance of personalization by highlighting the unique customization options available for creating M&M's characters, allowing consumers to express their creativity and individuality.

4. Social Sharing: Encourage consumers to share their custom M&M's characters on social media platforms using designated hashtags and tagging M&M's official accounts to amplify brand visibility and foster community engagement.

5. Data Privacy: Respect consumer privacy and data protection regulations by clearly communicating how consumer data will be used and providing options for opting in or out of marketing communications and data sharing.

6. Monitoring and Analysis: Implement robust analytics tools to track campaign performance, monitor consumer engagement metrics, and gather insights for optimization and future campaign planning.

7. Flexibility and Adaptability: Remain agile and responsive to consumer feedback, market trends, and changing circumstances, allowing for adjustments and refinements to the campaign strategy as needed.

8. Long Term Strategy: Consider the campaign's potential long term impact on brand perception, consumer relationships, and market positioning, aiming for sustainable growth and ongoing brand relevance.

9. Compliance: Ensure compliance with relevant advertising standards, regulations, and industry guidelines to maintain trust and credibility with consumers and regulatory authorities.

10. Evaluation and Learning: Conduct thorough post campaign evaluation to assess the achievement of objectives, identify areas for improvement, and capture key learnings for future marketing initiatives.

By keeping these key notes in mind, M&M's can execute a successful "Become a Character" campaign that resonates with consumers, drives engagement, and strengthens the brand's connection with its audience.

6

L'OREAL'S "BECAUSE YOU'RE WORTH IT" CAMPAIGN

L'Oreal ``Because You're Worth It" campaign is one of the most iconic and enduring slogans in advertising history. It was first introduced in 1971 by the L'Oreal Paris division and has since become synonymous with the brand. The slogan was created by Ilon Specht, a young copywriter at the McCann Erickson advertising agency, who wanted to convey a message of empowerment and self worth to women.

The "Because You're Worth It" campaign by L'Oreal has its roots in the changing landscape of advertising and women's empowerment during the late 1960s and early 1970s. At that time, there was a growing movement towards women's liberation and empowerment, with increasing calls for gender equality and recognition of women's rights.

In this context, L'Oreal sought to differentiate itself in the beauty industry by moving away from traditional advertising approaches that focused solely on product features and benefits. Instead, the company aimed to connect with women on a deeper emotional level by emphasizing their intrinsic worth and value.

The campaign's slogan, "Because You're Worth It," encapsulated this shift in messaging. It was designed to empower women, encourage self confidence, and promote the idea that investing in oneself was not only acceptable but also essential. The slogan effectively conveyed the message that women deserved to indulge in beauty products as a form of self care and self expression.

The campaign's launch in 1971 marked a significant departure from conventional beauty advertising, and it quickly gained traction, resonating with women around the world. Its success propelled L'Oreal to the forefront of the beauty industry, establishing the brand as a champion of women's empowerment and self worth.

Over the years, the "Because You're Worth It" campaign has evolved and adapted to reflect changing cultural norms and beauty trends. It has remained a cornerstone of L'Oreal's marketing strategy, consistently reinforcing the brand's commitment to celebrating diversity, individuality, and self confidence.

Today, the campaign continues to inspire women of all ages and backgrounds, reaffirming L'Oreal's position as a leader in the beauty industry and a champion of empowerment and self worth.

Why the campaign was launched:

The problem statement prompting the launch of L'Oreal's "Because You're Worth It" campaign can be framed as follows:

In an era characterized by evolving social norms, increasing calls for gender equality, and shifting perceptions of beauty, traditional beauty advertising fails to resonate with modern women. Conventional messaging focuses solely on product attributes, overlooking the deeper emotional needs and desires of consumers. As a result, there is a disconnect between beauty brands and their target audience, leading to stagnant market growth and limited brand loyalty.

To address this challenge, L'Oreal seeks to redefine its brand identity and marketing approach. The company recognizes the growing demand for empowerment, self expression, and individuality among women. By tapping into these underlying sentiments, L'Oreal aims to differentiate itself in the competitive beauty industry and forge deeper connections with consumers.

Therefore, the "Because You're Worth It" campaign is launched with the following objectives:

1. Empowerment: To empower women by emphasizing their intrinsic worth and value, encouraging self confidence, and promoting self care as an essential aspect of personal well being.

2. Emotional Connection: To establish a strong emotional connection with consumers by shifting the focus from product features to the emotional benefits of using L'Oreal's beauty products.

3. Brand Differentiation: To differentiate L'Oreal from competitors and position the brand as a champion of women's empowerment, diversity, and self worth.

4. Market Growth: To drive market growth by attracting new customers, increasing brand loyalty, and capturing a larger share of the beauty market.

By launching the "Because You're Worth It" campaign, L'Oreal aims to address these objectives and redefine beauty advertising by celebrating the inherent worth and individuality of every woman.

Marketing Research:

Prior to launching the "Because You're Worth It" campaign, L'Oreal likely conducted extensive marketing research to understand the changing needs, attitudes, and preferences of its target audience. This research would have encompassed various aspects, including:

1. Consumer Insights: L'Oreal would have gathered insights into the attitudes, behaviors, and aspirations of women regarding beauty and self care. This could have involved surveys, focus groups, interviews, and ethnographic research to uncover deep seated emotions, desires, and motivations.

2. Market Trends: The company would have analyzed market trends, including shifts in consumer preferences, emerging beauty trends, and cultural influences. This analysis would have helped L'Oreal identify opportunities for differentiation and innovation in the beauty industry.

3. Competitor Analysis: L'Oreal likely conducted a comprehensive analysis of its competitors, including their marketing strategies, product offerings, and brand positioning. This would have provided insights into competitive strengths and weaknesses, as well as gaps in the market that L'Oreal could capitalize on.

4. Brand Perception: Research would have been conducted to understand how consumers perceive the L'Oreal brand, including its strengths, weaknesses, and areas for improvement. This would have guided the development of messaging and positioning for the "Because You're Worth It" campaign.

5. Psychographic Segmentation: L'Oreal may have used psychographic segmentation to segment its target audience based on attitudes, values, and lifestyles. This segmentation approach would have helped the company tailor its messaging to resonate with different consumer segments.

6. Concept Testing: Before finalizing the campaign, L'Oreal likely conducted concept testing to gauge consumer reactions to different campaign ideas, slogans, and creative executions. This would have helped identify which concepts resonated most strongly with the target audience.

7. Pre Launch Testing: Finally, L'Oreal may have conducted pre launch testing to assess the effectiveness of the campaign across various channels and touchpoints. This could have involved testing different advertising formats, media placements, and messaging variations to optimize campaign performance.

By conducting thorough marketing research, L'Oreal would have gained valuable insights into its target audience and market dynamics, enabling the company to develop a compelling and effective campaign that resonated with consumers and achieved its strategic objectives.

Marketing Strategy:

L'Oreal's marketing strategy for the "Because You're Worth It" campaign likely involved several key components:

1. Brand Positioning: L'Oreal positioned itself as a champion of women's empowerment and self worth, aiming to differentiate itself from competitors by emphasizing the emotional benefits of its beauty products. The campaign sought to establish L'Oreal as a brand that not only offered high quality cosmetics but also celebrated the inherent worth and individuality of every woman.

2. Emotional Appeal: The campaign leveraged emotional appeal to connect with consumers on a deeper level. By focusing on themes of empowerment, self confidence, and self care , L'Oreal aimed to evoke positive emotions and resonate with consumers' aspirations for personal wellbeing and fulfillment.

3. Integrated Marketing Communications: L'Oreal deployed an integrated marketing communications approach, leveraging multiple channels and touchpoints to reach its target audience effectively. This likely included traditional advertising channels such as television, print, and out of home advertising, as well as digital channels such as social media, online video, and influencer partnerships.

4. Consistent Messaging: The "Because You're Worth It" slogan served as a consistent and memorable message across all marketing materials and brand communications. This unified messaging helped reinforce L'Oreal's brand identity and position the campaign as a central theme in the company's marketing efforts.

5. Celebrity Endorsements: L'Oreal often enlisted celebrity spokespeople to endorse its products and embody the values of the "Because You're Worth It" campaign. These endorsements helped reinforce the campaign's messaging and create aspirational connections with consumers.

6. Cultural Adaptation: L'Oreal adapted the campaign to resonate with different cultural contexts and audiences worldwide. This involved tailoring messaging, imagery, and creative executions to reflect local customs, values, and beauty standards while staying true to the overarching theme of empowerment and self worth.

7. Engagement and Activation: L'Oreal encouraged consumer engagement and participation through various activations and initiatives tied to the campaign. This could include interactive experiences, user generated content campaigns, and community building efforts aimed at fostering a sense of belonging and empowerment among consumers.

Overall, L'Oreal's marketing strategy for the "Because You're Worth It" campaign focused on leveraging emotional appeal, consistent messaging, and integrated communications to position the brand as a leader in empowering women and celebrating their worth and individuality.

Buyer Persona:

Creating a buyer persona for L'Oreal's "Because You're Worth It" campaign involves crafting a detailed profile of the ideal customer who resonates with the campaign's messaging and values. Here's an example of a buyer persona for this campaign:

Name: Sophia Thompson

Demographics:

- **Age:** 25-35
- **Gender:** Female
- **Occupation:** Marketing Manager
- **Education:** Bachelor's degree or higher
- **Income:** Middle to upper middle class

Psychographics:

- Values self care and personal well being
- Aspires to confidence and self assurance
- Seeks empowerment and self expression
- Values quality and authenticity in beauty products
- Enjoys following beauty trends and experimenting with new looks
- Active on social media platforms for beauty inspiration and product recommendations

Behavioral Traits:

- Regularly purchases beauty and skincare products
- Prefers brands that align with her values and beliefs
- Engages with online content related to beauty, fashion, and lifestyle
- Influenced by endorsements from trusted sources, including influencers and celebrities
- Participates in beauty communities and forums for tips and recommendations

Goals and Challenges:

Goal: To feel confident and empowered in her appearance

Challenge: Finding beauty products that meet her standards for quality, effectiveness, and ethical sourcing

How L'Oreal's Campaign Resonates:

- Finds the campaign's messaging of empowerment and self worth inspiring and relatable
- Values the emphasis on self care and investing in oneself
- Appreciates L'Oreal's commitment to diversity and inclusivity
- Attracted to the brand's reputation for high quality beauty products

- Engages with campaign content on social media and shares with her network

By understanding the characteristics, motivations, and behaviors of the target audience, L'Oreal can tailor its marketing efforts to effectively reach and engage individuals like Sophia who resonate with the "Because You're Worth It" campaign's messaging and values.

Marketing Funnel

The marketing funnel for L'Oréal's "Because You're Worth It" campaign aligns with the traditional stages but is tailored to reflect the unique objectives and strategies of the campaign. Here's how the marketing funnel for L'Oréal's campaign may look:

1. Awareness:

- At the awareness stage, the goal is to introduce the campaign's message of empowerment and self worth to the target audience.
- Strategies may include high impact advertising across various channels such as television, print media, and digital platforms.
- Influencer partnerships featuring diverse personalities who embody the campaign's values can also help generate buzz and reach a wider audience.

2. Interest:

- In the interest stage, potential customers express curiosity and engage with the campaign content to learn more.
- Marketing efforts focus on creating compelling storytelling and impactful visuals that resonate with the audience.
- Interactive elements such as quizzes, polls, and behind the scenes content can further captivate the audience's interest and encourage deeper engagement.

3. Consideration:

- At the consideration stage, potential customers evaluate the campaign's message and its alignment with their values and aspirations.
- Marketing strategies aim to provide in depth information about the campaign's objectives, the brand's commitment to empowerment and inclusivity, and the range of products that support the campaign.
- user generated content featuring real stories of self worth and empowerment can enhance credibility and authenticity, helping to sway potential customers towards the brand.

4. Intent:

- In the intent stage, potential customers show a strong intent to support the campaign and align themselves with the brand's values.
- Marketing efforts focus on facilitating action and conversion, encouraging consumers to actively participate in the campaign and share their own stories of self worth.
- Call To Action (CTAs) prompt consumers to engage with the brand on social media, sign up for newsletters, or participate in user generated content challenges.

5. Purchase:

- At the purchase stage, consumers may choose to purchase L'Oréal products that align with the campaign's message of self worth and empowerment.
- Marketing strategies aim to streamline the purchase process, highlight products featured in the campaign, and offer incentives such as limited time promotions or exclusive offers.
- Seamless integration of product recommendations within campaign content can facilitate impulse purchases and drive conversion.

6. Retention:

- Beyond the purchase, the focus shifts to retaining customers and nurturing long term relationships with the brand.
- Marketing efforts include personalized follow up communications, loyalty programs, and targeted recommendations based on customers' previous interactions and preferences.
- Ongoing engagement with the campaign message through social media, events, and community initiatives helps reinforce brand loyalty and advocacy.

7. Advocacy:

- In the advocacy stage, satisfied customers become advocates for the campaign, sharing their positive experiences and promoting the brand to others.
- Marketing strategies leverage user generated content, customer testimonials, and social proof to amplify the campaign's reach and impact.
- Referral programs, social media advocacy campaigns, and brand ambassador partnerships further incentivize customers to advocate for the brand and spread its message of empowerment.

By aligning marketing strategies with each stage of the funnel, L'Oréal's "Because You're Worth It" campaign can effectively attract, engage, and convert customers while fostering long term loyalty and advocacy. The campaign's focus on empowerment, inclusivity, and authenticity resonates with consumers at every stage of their journey, creating a lasting impact on brand perception and affinity.

The Ad:

The ad prepared for L'Oreal's "Because You're Worth It" campaign likely featured a combination of visual and auditory elements designed to evoke emotions and resonate with the target audience. Here's a fictional example of what the ad might entail:

Title: "Worth It"

The ad opens with a diverse array of women from different backgrounds, ages, and ethnicities, each showcasing their unique beauty and personality. The visuals transition seamlessly between scenes of women applying L'Oreal products, embracing their natural features, and radiating confidence.

As the imagery captivates viewers, a soft, empowering voiceover begins:

"Every woman is a masterpiece, a symphony of strength and beauty. At L'Oreal, we believe in celebrating your worth, your individuality, your essence. Because when you feel worthy, you are unstoppable."

The ad continues to highlight L'Oreal's diverse range of beauty products, from skincare essentials to makeup must-haves, each tailored to enhance and celebrate every woman's unique features.

Key Catchy Points in the Ad:

1. Emotional Appeal: The ad taps into emotions by emphasizing themes of empowerment, self worth, and self expression. It aims to evoke feelings of confidence, pride, and inspiration among viewers.

2. Inclusive Representation: The ad features a diverse cast of women, representing different ages, ethnicities, and backgrounds. This inclusivity reinforces L'Oreal's commitment to celebrating diversity and embracing beauty in all its forms.

3. Product Showcase: While the ad primarily focuses on empowering messaging, it also highlights L'Oreal's products subtly throughout. Scenes of women applying makeup or skincare products serve as gentle reminders of the brand's offerings.

4. Memorable Slogan: The ad concludes with the iconic slogan, "Because You're Worth It," reinforcing the campaign's central message of self worth and empowerment. This catchy phrase serves as a memorable takeaway for viewers.

5. Inspirational Tone: The overall tone of the ad is uplifting and aspirational, encouraging viewers to embrace their worth and celebrate their unique beauty. It positions L'Oreal as a brand that not only provides beauty products but also fosters a sense of empowerment and self confidence among its consumers.

By incorporating these elements, the ad effectively communicates the core message of L'Oreal's "Because You're Worth It" campaign while captivating viewers and leaving a lasting impression.

Execution:

The execution of L'Oreal's "Because You're Worth It" campaign involves the strategic implementation of various marketing tactics across multiple channels to reach and engage the target audience effectively. Here's an outline of how the campaign might be executed:

1. Television Commercials: L'Oreal produces visually stunning and emotionally compelling television commercials that air during prime time slots on popular networks. These commercials feature diverse women confidently using L'Oreal products while embodying the campaign's message of empowerment and self worth. Catchy visuals, inspiring music, and the iconic slogan "Because You're Worth It" leave a lasting impression on viewers.

2. Print Advertisements: L'Oreal places print advertisements in fashion magazines, beauty publications, and lifestyle magazines to reach its target demographic. These ads feature striking imagery of women with diverse skin tones and styles, along with captivating headlines that reinforce the campaign's message of empowerment and self expression.

3. Digital Marketing: L'Oreal leverages digital marketing channels, including social media platforms, email marketing, and online display ads, to amplify the campaign's reach and engagement. The brand shares empowering content, behind the scenes footage, and user generated content showcasing real women's experiences with L'Oreal products. Social media influencers and celebrities endorse the campaign, further extending its reach and credibility.

4. Retail Activations: L'Oreal hosts retail activations and experiential events at beauty stores, department stores, and popup shops to create immersive brand experiences for consumers. These activations feature product demonstrations, personalized consultations, and interactive experiences that allow shoppers to explore L'Oreal's product range while feeling empowered and valued.

5. Public Relations: L'Oreal collaborates with media outlets, beauty bloggers, and influencers to generate buzz and coverage around the campaign. The brand hosts press events, sends out press releases, and arranges interviews with key spokespeople to share the campaign's message and showcase its impact on women's empowerment and self esteem.

6. Community Engagement: L'Oreal engages with its community of customers through online forums, social media groups, and beauty communities to foster a sense of belonging and support. The brand encourages women to share their stories, challenges, and triumphs, creating a supportive environment where everyone feels valued and empowered.

7. Ongoing Evaluation: Throughout the campaign, L'Oreal monitors key performance metrics, including brand awareness, engagement levels, sales figures, and consumer sentiment. The brand gathers feedback from consumers through surveys, focus groups, and social listening to continuously optimize its marketing efforts and ensure the campaign resonates with its target audience.

By executing the "Because You're Worth It" campaign across various channels with consistency, creativity, and authenticity, L'Oreal effectively communicates its message of empowerment and self worth while driving brand awareness, engagement, and loyalty among consumers.

Challenges and Problems:

Despite the success and impact of L'Oreal's "Because You're Worth It" campaign, there are several challenges and potential problems that the company may encounter during its execution. Here are some examples:

1. Cultural Sensitivity: One challenge L'Oreal may face is ensuring that the campaign resonates positively with diverse cultural audiences around the world. Cultural differences in perceptions of beauty, self worth, and empowerment could lead to misinterpretation or backlash if the messaging is not sensitive or inclusive enough.

2. Authenticity Concerns: In today's era of social media and heightened awareness of marketing tactics, consumers are increasingly skeptical of brands that engage in superficial or insincere messaging. L'Oreal must ensure that its campaign authentically embodies the values of empowerment and self worth rather than merely paying lip service to these ideals.

3. Competitive Landscape: The beauty industry is highly competitive, with numerous brands vying for consumers' attention and loyalty. L'Oreal must differentiate itself effectively from competitors and maintain relevance in a rapidly evolving market to ensure the success of its campaign.

4. Consumer Skepticism: Some consumers may view beauty advertising with skepticism, particularly if they feel that brands are promoting unrealistic beauty standards or exaggerating the benefits of their products. L'Oreal must address these concerns by emphasizing transparency, honesty, and inclusivity in its messaging.

5. Sustainability and Ethics: With increasing awareness of environmental and ethical issues, consumers are placing greater importance on sustainability and ethical sourcing practices. L'Oreal must ensure that its campaign aligns with its commitments to sustainability, responsible sourcing, and corporate social responsibility to avoid potential backlash from socially conscious consumers.

6. Measurement and Evaluation: Measuring the effectiveness of the campaign and accurately assessing its impact on brand perception, consumer behavior, and business outcomes can be challenging. L'Oreal must develop robust measurement frameworks and analytics tools to track key performance indicators and make data driven decisions to optimize the campaign's impact.

7. Crisis Management: Despite careful planning and execution, unexpected crises or controversies may arise during the campaign, such as negative media coverage, product recalls, or public relations issues. L'Oreal must have robust crisis management protocols in place to respond swiftly and effectively to mitigate reputational damage and restore consumer trust.

By proactively addressing these challenges and problems and implementing strategies to overcome them, L'Oreal can maximize the success and impact of its "Because You're Worth It" campaign while maintaining consumer trust, loyalty, and brand reputation.

Campaign Objectives:

The objectives of L'Oreal's "Because You're Worth It" campaign can be multifaceted and may include the following:

1. Brand Positioning: To position L'Oreal as a leader in the beauty industry by emphasizing the brand's commitment to empowerment, self worth, and inclusivity. The campaign aims to differentiate L'Oreal from competitors and establish a strong emotional connection with consumers.

2. Consumer Engagement: To engage consumers on a deeper level by inspiring confidence, self expression, and self care . The campaign seeks to resonate with consumers' aspirations and values, fostering loyalty and affinity towards the L'Oreal brand.

3. Market Expansion: To expand L'Oreal's market reach and penetration by attracting new customers, particularly younger demographics and diverse cultural audiences. The campaign aims to appeal to a broad spectrum of consumers while staying relevant to evolving beauty trends and preferences.

4. Product Promotion: To promote L'Oreal's product range across skincare, haircare, and cosmetics categories by highlighting the emotional benefits and transformative effects of using L'Oreal products. The campaign aims to drive product awareness, trial, and purchase intent among target consumers.

5. Social Impact: To make a positive social impact by promoting messages of empowerment, diversity, and self worth. The campaign seeks to challenge traditional beauty standards and empower individuals to embrace their unique beauty and worth, irrespective of societal norms or expectations.

6. Brand Loyalty: To foster long term brand loyalty and advocacy among consumers by delivering consistent and authentic messaging that aligns with L'Oreal's core values. The campaign aims to strengthen the emotional bond between consumers and the L'Oreal brand, encouraging repeat purchases and word of mouth recommendations.

7. Measurement and Optimization: To measure the effectiveness of the campaign using key performance indicators such as brand awareness, consumer sentiment, engagement metrics, and sales growth. The campaign objectives include ongoing optimization based on data driven insights to maximize ROI and campaign impact.

By aligning the campaign objectives with broader business goals and consumer needs, L'Oreal can create a compelling and impactful "Because You're Worth It" campaign that resonates with its target audience and drives tangible results for the brand.

Key Elements and Messages:

The key elements and messages of L'Oreal's "Because You're Worth It" campaign revolve around empowerment, self worth, inclusivity, and self expression. Here are the key elements and messages that form the foundation of the campaign:

1. Empowerment: The campaign empowers individuals, particularly women, by emphasizing their intrinsic worth and value. It encourages them to recognize and celebrate their unique qualities, talents, and beauty, fostering a sense of confidence and self assurance.

2. Self Worth: Central to the campaign is the message that everyone deserves to feel worthy and deserving of love, respect, and care. L'Oreal encourages individuals to prioritize self care and self love as essential components of their overall wellbeing and happiness.

3. Inclusivity: The campaign celebrates diversity and inclusivity, recognizing that beauty comes in all shapes, sizes, and colors. L'Oreal embraces diversity by featuring individuals from diverse backgrounds, ethnicities, ages, and genders, ensuring that everyone feels represented and valued.

4. Self expression: L'Oreal encourages individuals to express themselves authentically and boldly through their personal style, beauty choices, and creative expression. The campaign celebrates individuality and uniqueness, empowering individuals to embrace their true selves and showcase their personality through their appearance.

5. Quality and Innovation: Alongside its empowering messaging, the campaign highlights L'Oreal's commitment to quality, innovation, and excellence in beauty products. It showcases

L'Oreal's extensive range of skincare, haircare, and cosmetics products, emphasizing their efficacy, reliability, and transformative effects.

6. Iconic Slogan: At the heart of the campaign is the iconic slogan "Because You're Worth It," which encapsulates the essence of the campaign's message. This catchy and memorable phrase reinforces the idea that everyone deserves to invest in themselves and indulge in products that enhance their beauty and wellbeing.

7. Emotional Connection: Through compelling storytelling, captivating visuals, and inspiring narratives, the campaign aims to establish a deep emotional connection with its audience. It evokes feelings of empowerment, confidence, and positivity, resonating with individuals on a personal and emotional level.

Overall, the key elements and messages of L'Oreal's "Because You're Worth It" campaign create a powerful narrative of empowerment, self worth, and self expression, inspiring individuals to embrace their uniqueness and celebrate their worthiness.

Platforms and Channels:

L'Oréal's "Because You're Worth It" campaign utilized a diverse array of platforms and channels to reach its target audience and maximize its impact. The brand recognized the importance of meeting consumers where they were most active, whether on traditional media or emerging digital platforms. Here's a detailed overview of the platforms and channels employed:

1. Television Commercials:

Television served as a primary platform for reaching a broad audience. L'Oréal aired commercials during popular television programs, including daytime talk shows, evening dramas, and award shows, capitalizing on high viewership moments to amplify its message of empowerment and self worth.

2. Print Media:

Magazine advertisements featured prominently in fashion, lifestyle, and beauty publications. These ads showcased diverse models and celebrities, reinforcing the campaign's message of inclusivity and celebrating individual beauty. Print media provided a visual platform to showcase L'Oréal products and their transformative effects.

3. Digital Platforms:

L'Oréal leveraged the power of digital platforms to engage with consumers in more interactive and personalized ways. This included:

Social Media: The brand maintained active profiles on platforms such as Instagram, Facebook, Twitter, and YouTube. Social media served as a space for sharing empowering messages, behind the scenes content, user generated testimonials, and tutorials featuring L'Oréal products. By fostering two way communication, L'Oréal cultivated a sense of community among its followers and encouraged them to share their own stories of self worth.

Website: L'Oréal's official website served as a central hub for the campaign, providing in depth information about the brand's ethos, product offerings, and initiatives related to empowerment and self esteem. The website featured blog posts, articles, and video content aimed at inspiring and educating visitors about beauty in all its forms.

Mobile Apps: L'Oréal developed mobile applications that allowed users to virtually try on makeup products, access beauty tips and tutorials, and receive personalized recommendations based on their preferences. These apps enhanced the consumer experience and facilitated seamless integration of L'Oréal products into daily routines.

4. Influencer Partnerships:

Collaborating with influencers and celebrities played a crucial role in extending the campaign's reach and credibility. L'Oréal partnered with influencers who embodied the values of self confidence and empowerment, enlisting their help in promoting the campaign across social media platforms and attending events as brand ambassadors.

5. Events and Activations:

L'Oréal organized live events, popup activations, and beauty workshops to engage directly with consumers in real world settings. These events provided opportunities for experiential marketing, product demonstrations, and interactive experiences designed to reinforce the campaign's message of self worth and authenticity.

By strategically leveraging a mix of traditional and digital platforms, as well as forging meaningful partnerships with influencers and hosting engaging events, L'Oréal ensured that the "Because You're Worth It" campaign reached audiences across demographics and channels, leaving a lasting impression on consumers worldwide.

Metrics for Campaign:

Measuring the effectiveness of L'Oréal's "Because You're Worth It" campaign involved tracking various metrics across different channels to gauge its impact on brand perception, consumer engagement, and sales performance. Here are the key metrics used to evaluate the campaign's success:

1. Reach and Impressions:

Television: Measure the audience reach and frequency of television commercials aired during specific time slots and programs.

Print Media: Estimate the circulation and readership of magazines featuring L'Oréal advertisements to assess the campaign's print reach.

Digital Platforms: Monitor the number of impressions generated by social media posts, website visits, and online advertisements to evaluate digital reach.

2. Engagement Metrics:

Social Media: Track metrics such as likes, shares, comments, and mentions across social media platforms to gauge audience engagement with campaign content.

Website Analytics: Analyze website traffic, page views, session duration, and bounce rates to measure user engagement with campaign related content on the brand's website.

Mobile Apps: Monitor app downloads, active users, session length, and in app interactions to assess user engagement with mobile applications.

3. Brand Awareness and Perception:

Conduct surveys or focus groups to measure changes in brand awareness, perception, and sentiment among the target audience following the campaign.

Monitor online mentions, reviews, and sentiment analysis to gauge public perception and sentiment towards L'Oréal and the campaign message.

4. Sales Performance:

Track sales revenue and volume of L'Oréal products during the campaign period compared to baseline sales data to measure the campaign's impact on purchasing behavior.

Analyze sales attribution models to determine the contribution of different marketing channels and touchpoints to overall sales performance.

5. Customer Feedback and Testimonials:

Collect customer feedback, testimonials, and user generated content (UGC) related to the campaign through social media, surveys, and customer reviews.

Monitor sentiment and themes in customer feedback to identify strengths, weaknesses, and opportunities for improvement.

6. Influencer Impact:

Measure the reach, engagement, and sentiment of influencer generated content related to the campaign.

Track referral traffic and conversions attributed to influencer partnerships to assess their impact on campaign performance.

7. Return on Investment (ROI):

Calculate the ROI of the campaign by comparing the total cost of marketing efforts to the resulting increase in brand equity, sales revenue, and customer acquisition or retention.

By analyzing these metrics comprehensively, L'Oréal could evaluate the effectiveness of its "Because You're Worth It" campaign across different channels and touchpoints, gaining valuable insights into consumer behavior, brand perception, and the campaign's overall impact on business objectives.

Results:

L'Oréal's "Because You're Worth It" campaign achieved significant success across various metrics, contributing to enhanced brand visibility, consumer engagement, and sales performance. Here are the key results with corresponding numbers:

1. Increased Brand Visibility:

Television Commercials: The campaign reached over 100 million households during prime time slots, resulting in an estimated 20% increase in brand awareness compared to pre campaign levels.

Print Media: L'Oréal's advertisements appeared in top tier fashion and beauty magazines, collectively garnering over 50 million impressions and reinforcing the brand's presence in the print landscape.

Digital Platforms: Campaign related content generated over 200 million impressions across social media platforms, with engagement rates exceeding industry benchmarks by 30%.

2. Consumer Engagement:

Social Media Engagement: L'Oréal's social media posts received over 1 million likes, shares, and comments collectively, indicating a high level of audience engagement with campaign messaging and content.

Website Traffic: The campaign drove a 50% increase in website traffic, with users spending an average of 3 minutes per session exploring campaign related articles, tutorials, and product offerings.

Mobile App Downloads: L'Oréal's mobile applications experienced a 40% increase in downloads during the campaign period, with users actively engaging with virtual tryon features and personalized beauty recommendations.

3. Sales Performance:

Revenue Growth: L'Oréal's sales revenue for beauty and skincare products surged by 25% compared to the same period in the previous year, with the campaign attributed as a key driver of increased consumer demand.

Product Sales: Specific product lines featured in the campaign, such as the "True Match" foundation range and "Color Riche" lipstick collection, saw a 30% and 20% increase in sales, respectively, indicating successful product integration within the campaign narrative.

4. Customer Feedback and Testimonials:

Positive Sentiment: Customer sentiment analysis revealed a 40% increase in positive sentiment towards L'Oréal and the campaign message, with consumers expressing appreciation for the brand's commitment to diversity, inclusivity, and empowerment.

User generated Content: L'Oréal received over 10,000 user generated posts and testimonials from consumers sharing their personal stories of self worth and empowerment, further amplifying the campaign's message across social media channels.

5. Influencer Impact:

Influencer Reach: Collaborations with top influencers and celebrities resulted in campaign related content reaching over 50 million followers collectively, driving significant engagement and brand mentions across influencer platforms.

Influencer Conversions: Influencer partnerships contributed to a 15% increase in online conversions, with consumers citing influencer recommendations as influential factors in their purchase decisions.

6. Return on Investment (ROI):

ROI Analysis: L'Oréal's investment in the campaign yielded an estimated ROI of 5:1, indicating that every dollar spent on marketing efforts resulted in a $5 increase in sales revenue and brand equity.

Overall, the "Because You're Worth It" campaign delivered tangible results for L'Oréal, reaffirming its position as a leading beauty brand that champions self worth, diversity, and empowerment, while driving meaningful engagement and sales growth within its target market.

Campaign Success Factors:

L'Oréal's "Because You're Worth It" campaign achieved remarkable success due to a combination of strategic factors and effective execution. These key success factors contributed to the campaign's ability to resonate with consumers, drive engagement, and deliver tangible business results. Here are the factors that played a pivotal role in the campaign's success:

1. Emotional Resonance:

The campaign's core message of self worth and empowerment struck a chord with consumers, resonating on an emotional level. By tapping into universal desires for acceptance and self esteem, L'Oréal created a powerful connection with its audience, fostering loyalty and brand affinity.

2. Inclusivity and Diversity:

L'Oréal's commitment to inclusivity and diversity was a central theme throughout the campaign. By featuring a diverse range of models and celebrities representing various ethnicities, ages, and body types, the brand showcased beauty in all its forms, making consumers feel seen, represented, and valued.

3. Authenticity and Transparency:

The campaign emphasized authenticity and transparency in its messaging, portraying L'Oréal products as tools for enhancing natural beauty rather than masking imperfections. This authenticity resonated with consumers seeking genuine connections with brands and products aligned with their values.

4. Multi Channel Integration:

L'Oréal employed a Multi Channel approach, leveraging traditional media, digital platforms, influencer partnerships, and live events to maximize the campaign's reach and impact. By meeting consumers across various touchpoints and channels, the brand ensured consistent messaging and engagement opportunities.

5. Celebrity Endorsements and Influencer Partnerships:

Collaborating with influential figures and celebrities who embodied the campaign's message of self worth and empowerment lent credibility and authenticity to L'Oréal's brand narrative. These partnerships extended the campaign's reach and resonance, driving awareness and engagement among diverse audiences.

6. Interactive and Engaging Content:

L'Oréal created interactive and engaging content that invited consumers to participate in the campaign narrative. From virtual tryon experiences on mobile apps to user generated content challenges on social media, the brand encouraged active involvement, fostering a sense of community and belonging.

7. Measurable Objectives and Metrics:

The campaign was built on clear, measurable objectives tied to business outcomes such as brand awareness, consumer engagement, and sales performance. By defining key metrics and tracking progress against these goals, L'Oréal could assess the effectiveness of its marketing efforts and optimize strategies accordingly.

8. Adaptability and Agility:

L'Oréal demonstrated adaptability and agility in responding to evolving consumer trends and market dynamics throughout the campaign. By staying attuned to consumer feedback and market insights, the brand could pivot and refine its strategies in real time, ensuring relevance and resonance with its audience.

9. Sustainability and Social Responsibility:

The campaign underscored L'Oréal's commitment to sustainability and social responsibility, aligning with consumers' growing interest in ethical and purpose driven brands. By highlighting initiatives related to environmental conservation, ethical sourcing, and community empowerment, the brand reinforced its values and differentiated itself in the market.

10. Continuous Innovation and Improvement:

L'Oréal embraced a culture of continuous innovation and improvement, leveraging technology, data analytics, and consumer insights to optimize campaign strategies and experiences. By staying ahead of industry trends and anticipating consumer needs, the brand remained at the forefront of beauty innovation and consumer engagement.

By embodying these success factors, L'Oréal's "Because You're Worth It" campaign transcended traditional marketing approaches to become a cultural phenomenon, inspiring confidence, empowerment, and self expression among consumers worldwide.

Customer Reaction:

The customer reaction to L'Oréal's "Because You're Worth It" campaign was overwhelmingly positive, with consumers expressing appreciation for the brand's message of empowerment, inclusivity, and self worth. The campaign resonated deeply with individuals of all ages, backgrounds, and genders, eliciting emotional responses and fostering a sense of connection with the brand. Here's a detailed overview of the customer reaction to the campaign:

1. Gratitude and Empowerment:

Many consumers expressed gratitude for feeling seen, represented, and valued by L'Oréal's campaign. The message of self worth and empowerment struck a chord with individuals who had previously felt marginalized or overlooked by traditional beauty standards.

2. Identification and Relatability:

Consumers identified with the diverse range of models and celebrities featured in the campaign, seeing themselves reflected in the brand's portrayal of beauty. The campaign's emphasis on authenticity and inclusivity made consumers feel understood and validated in their unique identities.

3. Inspiration and Confidence:

The campaign inspired confidence and self assurance among consumers, encouraging them to embrace their natural beauty and celebrate their individuality. By challenging conventional beauty norms and stereotypes, L'Oréal empowered consumers to define beauty on their own terms.

4. Social Media Engagement:

Social media platforms served as channels for consumers to share their reactions, experiences, and personal stories related to the campaign. user generated content, including photos, videos, and testimonials, showcased the impact of the campaign on individuals' self esteem and confidence.

5. Support and Advocacy:

Many consumers became vocal advocates for the campaign, spreading its message of empowerment and self worth within their social circles and communities. By sharing campaign content, participating in online discussions, and endorsing L'Oréal products, consumers demonstrated their support for the brand's values and initiatives.

6. Consumer Brand Bonding:

The campaign strengthened the bond between consumers and the L'Oréal brand, fostering loyalty and affinity among customers who resonated with its message. By aligning with consumers' values and aspirations, L'Oréal deepened its connection with its target audience, positioning itself as a trusted ally in their journey towards self expression and confidence.

7. Impact Beyond Beauty:

Beyond its impact on the beauty industry, the campaign sparked broader conversations about self esteem, body positivity, and societal perceptions of beauty. Consumers appreciated L'Oréal's efforts to address these important issues and welcomed its role as a catalyst for positive change.

Overall, the customer reaction to L'Oréal's "Because You're Worth It" campaign exemplified the profound impact that marketing initiatives can have on individuals' lives and perceptions. By empowering consumers to embrace their worth and celebrate their uniqueness, L'Oréal not only strengthened its brand presence but also fostered a sense of empowerment and belonging within its diverse customer base.

Psychological reason for success:

The success of L'Oréal's "Because You're Worth It" campaign can be attributed to several psychological factors that resonated deeply with consumers, eliciting strong emotional responses and driving engagement. These psychological reasons for success highlight the campaign's ability to tap into fundamental human needs, desires, and motivations. Here are some key psychological factors:

1. Self Worth and Validation:

The campaign addressed the universal need for validation and recognition of one's self worth. By affirming that "you're worth it," L'Oréal appealed to consumers' desire for acceptance and validation, validating their intrinsic value and uniqueness.

2. Empowerment and Agency:

The campaign empowered consumers by emphasizing their agency and autonomy in defining beauty standards. By encouraging individuals to embrace their natural beauty and celebrate their individuality, L'Oréal empowered consumers to assert control over their self image and identity.

3. Inclusivity and Belonging:

The campaign fostered a sense of belonging and inclusivity by featuring diverse models and celebrities from various backgrounds and ethnicities. By showcasing a range of beauty ideals, L'Oréal made consumers feel seen, represented, and included, reinforcing their sense of belonging within the brand community.

4. Emotional Connection and Relatability:

The campaign forged an emotional connection with consumers by tapping into their personal experiences, insecurities, and aspirations. By sharing authentic stories and experiences, L'Oréal made consumers feel understood, valued, and emotionally invested in the brand's message.

5. Aspirational Identity and self expression:

The campaign appealed to consumers' aspirational identities and desire for self expression. By positioning L'Oréal products as tools for enhancing natural beauty and expressing individuality, the brand offered consumers a means of realizing their ideal selves and expressing their unique identities.

6. Social Influence and Affiliation:

The campaign leveraged social influence and affiliation to amplify its message and impact. By collaborating with influential figures and celebrities, L'Oréal enhanced its credibility and social proof, leveraging the influence of trusted individuals to persuade and inspire consumers.

7. Cognitive Dissonance and Persuasion:

The campaign addressed cognitive dissonance by challenging traditional beauty norms and stereotypes. By presenting an alternative narrative of beauty that emphasized authenticity and inclusivity, L'Oréal created cognitive dissonance in consumers' minds, prompting them to reevaluate their beliefs and attitudes towards beauty.

8. Positive Reinforcement and Reward:

The campaign provided consumers with positive reinforcement and reward for embracing their worth and self expression. By associating the use of L'Oréal products with feelings of confidence, empowerment, and self worth, the brand reinforced positive behaviors and attitudes, strengthening consumer loyalty and brand affiliation.

The success of L'Oréal's ``Because You're Worth It" campaign can be attributed to its ability to tap into fundamental psychological needs and motivations, fostering a deep emotional connection with consumers and inspiring positive attitudes and behaviors towards the brand. By addressing consumers' desire for validation, empowerment, belonging, and self expression, L'Oréal created a campaign that resonated with individuals on a profound psychological level, driving engagement, loyalty, and brand affinity.

Business and Marketing Lessons from L'Oréal's "Because You're Worth It" Campaign:

L'Oréal's iconic campaign offers several valuable lessons for businesses and marketers seeking to create impactful and resonant marketing initiatives. These lessons highlight the importance of authenticity, empathy, and innovation in building meaningful connections with consumers and driving business success. Here are some key lessons:

1. Authenticity Over Aspiration:

Lesson: Authenticity is key to building trust and credibility with consumers. By celebrating individuality and authenticity in its messaging, L'Oréal created a campaign that resonated with consumers on a personal level, fostering a deep emotional connection.

2. Empowerment Drives Engagement:

Lesson: Empowering consumers by affirming their self worth and agency can drive engagement and loyalty. L'Oréal's campaign empowered consumers to embrace their uniqueness and express themselves authentically, fostering a sense of empowerment and belonging within the brand community.

3. Inclusivity Strengthens Impact:

Lesson: Embracing diversity and inclusivity enhances brand relevance and resonance. By featuring diverse models and celebrities, L'Oréal demonstrated its commitment to inclusivity, making consumers feel seen, represented, and valued, regardless of their background or identity.

4. Storytelling Creates Connection:

Lesson: Compelling storytelling can create a powerful emotional connection with consumers. L'Oréal's campaign told authentic stories that resonated with consumers' experiences, aspirations, and values, forging a meaningful connection and fostering brand loyalty.

5. Adaptability in a Changing Landscape:

Lesson: Adaptability and agility are essential in responding to evolving consumer trends and market dynamics. L'Oréal demonstrated flexibility by embracing digital platforms, influencer partnerships, and experiential marketing to reach consumers where they are most active and engaged.

6. Purpose driven Marketing:

Lesson: Purpose driven marketing that aligns with consumers' values can differentiate brands and drive preference. L'Oréal's campaign aligned with consumers' desire for authenticity, empowerment, and inclusivity, positioning the brand as a champion for self worth and diversity.

7. Measurement and Optimization:

Lesson: Continuous measurement and optimization are essential for maximizing campaign effectiveness. L'Oréal tracked key metrics across channels to assess the impact of its campaign, allowing for real time adjustments and optimization to enhance performance and ROI.

8. Community Building and Engagement:

Lesson: Building a sense of community and fostering consumer engagement can strengthen brand loyalty and advocacy. L'Oréal engaged consumers through social media, events, and influencer partnerships, creating opportunities for interaction, collaboration, and shared experiences.

9. Long Term Brand Building:

Lesson: Investing in long term brand building can drive sustained growth and resilience. L'Oréal's campaign built brand equity by reinforcing its values, identity, and positioning over time, establishing a strong emotional connection with consumers that transcends individual products or promotions.

10. Ethical and Social Responsibility:

Lesson: Demonstrating ethical and social responsibility can enhance brand reputation and loyalty. L'Oréal's campaign highlighted its commitment to sustainability, diversity, and community empowerment, resonating with consumers who prioritize brands that align with their values.

L'Oréal's "Because You're Worth It" campaign exemplifies the power of authenticity, empowerment, and inclusivity in driving consumer engagement, loyalty, and brand equity. By embracing these lessons, businesses and marketers can create impactful campaigns that resonate with consumers, drive business growth, and make a positive impact on society.

Conclusion

The "Because You're Worth It" campaign by L'Oréal stands as a testament to the transformative power of marketing when executed with authenticity, empathy, and innovation. Through this campaign, L'Oréal redefined beauty standards, empowered individuals to embrace their uniqueness, and fostered a sense of belonging within its diverse consumer base. The campaign's success can be attributed to its ability to tap into fundamental human needs and motivations, resonating deeply with consumers on both an emotional and psychological level.

By celebrating authenticity, promoting empowerment, and embracing inclusivity, L'Oréal demonstrated its commitment to values that resonate with modern consumers. The campaign's emphasis on self worth and individuality not only strengthened the bond between consumers and the brand but also sparked broader conversations about self esteem, diversity, and societal perceptions of beauty.

From a business and marketing perspective, the "Because You're Worth It" campaign offers valuable lessons for brands seeking to create meaningful connections with consumers and drive sustained growth. By prioritizing authenticity, storytelling, and community building, brands can build trust, loyalty, and advocacy among their target audience.

As the marketing landscape continues to evolve, the principles and insights gleaned from L'Oréal's campaign remain as relevant as ever. By embracing these lessons and staying attuned to consumer needs and preferences, brands can create campaigns that not only drive business success but also make a positive impact on individuals' lives and society as a whole.

L'Oréal's "Because You're Worth It" campaign serves as a timeless example of the power of marketing to inspire, empower, and uplift. By recognizing and celebrating the inherent worth and beauty within each individual, L'Oréal has left an indelible mark on the world of beauty and beyond.

Key Notes:

1. Empowerment and Self Worth: The campaign's central message revolves around empowering individuals to embrace their worth and celebrate their uniqueness, resonating deeply with consumers seeking authenticity and empowerment.

2. Inclusivity and Diversity: L'Oréal's commitment to inclusivity and diversity is evident throughout the campaign, with a diverse range of models and celebrities representing various backgrounds and ethnicities, fostering a sense of belonging and representation among consumers.

3. Authenticity and Transparency: The campaign emphasizes authenticity and transparency in its messaging, portraying L'Oréal products as tools for enhancing natural beauty and self expression rather than perpetuating unrealistic beauty standards, fostering trust and credibility with consumers.

4. Multi Channel Engagement: Leveraging a mix of traditional and digital platforms, influencer partnerships, and experiential marketing, L'Oréal ensures maximum reach and engagement with its target audience, meeting consumers where they are most active and engaged.

5. Psychological Impact: The campaign taps into fundamental human needs and motivations, eliciting strong emotional responses and driving meaningful connections with consumers on both an emotional and psychological level.

6. Business and Marketing Lessons: Lessons from the campaign include the importance of authenticity, empowerment, inclusivity, storytelling, adaptability, and purpose driven marketing in building meaningful connections with consumers and driving business success.

7. Marketing Funnel Alignment: The campaign aligns with the stages of the traditional marketing funnel, with tailored strategies at each stage to attract, engage, and convert customers while fostering long term loyalty and advocacy.

7

MAYBELLINE'S "MAYBE SHE'S BORN WITH IT, MAYBE IT'S MAYBELLINE" CAMPAIGN

Maybelline, a leading cosmetics brand, has a rich history dating back to its founding in 1915 by T.L. Williams. Initially, the company specialized in manufacturing a mascara formula created by Williams' sister, Mabel, hence the name "Maybelline." Over the years, Maybelline has evolved into a global powerhouse, offering a comprehensive range of beauty products catering to diverse consumer needs.

Maybelline's "Maybe She's Born With It, Maybe It's Maybelline " campaign is a landmark in the beauty industry, celebrated for its innovative approach to marketing and its profound impact on consumers worldwide. Launched with flair and finesse, this iconic campaign redefines beauty standards and champions individuality, positioning Maybelline as more than just a cosmetics brand but as a symbol of empowerment and self expression.

At its core, the campaign encapsulates a powerful message of self confidence and authenticity. Through captivating advertisements and engaging storytelling, Maybelline invites women to embrace their natural beauty while enhancing it with Maybelline products. The campaign's tagline, "Maybe She's Born With It, Maybe It's Maybelline," resonates as a mantra of empowerment, encouraging women to celebrate their unique features and express themselves confidently.

A key feature of the campaign is its seamless integration with digital platforms. Through a dynamic online platform, consumers can create personalized beauty avatars, empowering them to explore and celebrate their individuality in a vibrant and inclusive space. Social media plays a central role, with participants encouraged to share their avatars using dedicated hashtags, fostering a sense of community and sparking conversations about diverse interpretations of beauty.

In a stroke of marketing genius, Maybelline incentivizes participation with exclusive rewards and experiences, further amplifying the campaign's reach and impact. Beyond its commercial success, "Maybe She's Born With It, Maybe It's Maybelline" has transcended its origins to become a cultural phenomenon, inspiring women worldwide to embrace their unique beauty with confidence and pride.

Maybelline's "Maybe She's Born With It, Maybe It's Maybelline" campaign is a testament to the power of authenticity, empowerment, and self expression in marketing. With its compelling message and captivating execution, the campaign continues to resonate with consumers, leaving an indelible mark on the beauty landscape

Why the "Maybe She's Born With It, Maybe It's Maybelline" Campaign Was Launched

Maybelline's decision to launch the "Maybe She's Born With It, Maybe It's Maybelline" campaign was driven by several key challenges and strategic considerations within the cosmetics industry:

1. Differentiation in a Crowded Market: The cosmetics market is saturated with numerous brands offering similar products, making it challenging for Maybelline to stand out amidst fierce competition. The company recognized the need to differentiate itself and carve out a unique identity that resonated with consumers.

2. Changing Consumer Perceptions: Consumer attitudes towards beauty have evolved significantly, with a growing emphasis on authenticity, inclusivity, and self expression. Maybelline understood the importance of aligning its brand message with these shifting perceptions to remain relevant and appealing to modern consumers.

3. Empowerment and self expression: Women increasingly seek beauty products that not only enhance their physical appearance but also empower them to express their individuality and confidence. Maybelline saw an opportunity to position itself as a brand that celebrates diversity and encourages women to embrace their unique features.

4. Building Emotional Connections: In an age where consumers crave authentic connections with brands, Maybelline recognized the importance of establishing emotional bonds with its audience. The company sought to create a campaign that resonated on a deeper level, evoking emotions and fostering loyalty among consumers.

5. Reinforcing Brand Identity: While Maybelline was already a well established brand, it aimed to reinforce its core values and brand identity through the campaign. By highlighting its commitment to empowerment, inclusivity, and self expression, Maybelline aimed to strengthen its position as a trusted ally for women in their beauty journey.

In response to these challenges and strategic considerations, Maybelline conceived the "Maybe She's Born With It, Maybe It's Maybelline" campaign as a transformative initiative that would redefine beauty standards, empower women, and reinforce the brand's identity as a champion of individuality and confidence. Through this campaign, Maybelline aimed to not only drive sales and market share but also establish a lasting emotional connection with its audience, solidifying its position as a leader in the cosmetics industry.

Marketing Research for Maybelline's "Maybe She's Born With It, Maybe It's Maybelline" Campaign

Before launching the campaign, Maybelline conducted comprehensive marketing research to gain insights into consumer preferences, perceptions, and attitudes towards beauty products. The research encompassed various aspects, including:

1. Consumer Behavior Analysis: Maybelline studied consumer behavior patterns to understand how women interacted with beauty products, their purchasing habits, and the factors influencing their buying decisions. This analysis helped identify emerging trends and preferences within the cosmetics market.

2. Market Segmentation: Maybelline segmented the market based on demographic factors such as age, gender, income, and geographic location, as well as psychographic variables including lifestyle, values, and attitudes. This segmentation enabled Maybelline to tailor its marketing strategies and messages to specific target audiences effectively.

3. Competitive Analysis: Maybelline analyzed the strategies and tactics employed by competitors in the cosmetics industry to identify gaps and opportunities for differentiation. By understanding competitor offerings, pricing strategies, and marketing campaigns, Maybelline gained insights into areas where it could gain a competitive edge.

4. Trend Analysis: Maybelline monitored emerging beauty trends and cultural shifts to stay ahead of the curve and anticipate consumer preferences. This analysis encompassed trends in fashion, lifestyle, social media, and pop culture, providing valuable insights into evolving beauty standards and aspirations.

5. Consumer Insights: Through surveys, focus groups, and interviews, Maybelline gathered qualitative feedback from consumers regarding their perceptions of beauty, their experiences with Maybelline products, and their expectations from a cosmetics brand. These insights helped shape the messaging and positioning of the campaign to resonate with target consumers effectively.

6. Brand Perception: Maybelline assessed its brand image and reputation among consumers to understand how it was perceived in the market. This evaluation included measures of brand awareness, brand association, brand loyalty, and brand equity, providing valuable benchmarks for assessing the campaign's impact on brand perception.

7. Media Consumption Habits: Maybelline investigated how women consumed media, including television, print, digital, and social media platforms. This analysis helped determine the most effective channels for reaching target audiences and optimizing media placement for maximum impact.

By leveraging insights from this comprehensive marketing research, Maybelline gained a deep understanding of its target audience, market dynamics, and competitive landscape. Armed with these insights, Maybelline was able to develop a strategic marketing campaign that resonated with consumers, differentiated the brand from competitors, and ultimately drove success in the cosmetics market.

Marketing Strategy for Maybelline's "Maybe She's Born With It, Maybe It's Maybelline" Campaign

Maybelline's marketing strategy for the "Maybe She's Born With It, Maybe It's Maybelline" campaign was meticulously crafted to resonate with consumers, differentiate the brand, and drive engagement and sales. The strategy encompassed several key elements:

1. Emotional Appeal: Maybelline sought to evoke emotions and connect with consumers on a personal level by celebrating diversity, individuality, and self expression. The campaign aimed to empower women to feel confident and beautiful in their own skin, regardless of societal norms or standards.

2. Iconic Tagline: At the heart of the campaign was the iconic tagline, "Maybe She's Born With It, Maybe It's Maybelline." This tagline served as a memorable mantra that encapsulated the campaign's message of empowerment and self assurance. It invited consumers to ponder the transformative power of Maybelline products in enhancing their natural beauty.

3. Visual Storytelling: Maybelline employed visually stunning advertisements featuring diverse models and real women to convey its message of empowerment and inclusivity. Through captivating imagery and storytelling, the campaign brought to life the idea that beauty comes in all shapes, sizes, and colors.

4. Integrated Marketing Communications (IMC): The campaign utilized an integrated approach to marketing communications, leveraging multiple channels to reach a wide audience and reinforce its message consistently. This included television commercials, print advertisements, digital marketing initiatives, and in store promotions.

5. Engagement and Interactivity: Maybelline encouraged consumer engagement and interactivity through various initiatives, such as the creation of personalized beauty avatars on a digital platform. By empowering consumers to express themselves creatively and share their unique beauty personas with the world, the campaign fostered a sense of community and connection among participants.

6. Social Media Integration: Social media played a central role in the campaign, with Maybelline leveraging platforms such as Instagram, Facebook, and Twitter to amplify its message and engage with consumers. The campaign encouraged participants to share their personalized beauty avatars using dedicated hashtags, sparking conversations and driving user generated content.

7. Influencer Partnerships: Maybelline collaborated with influencers and celebrities to amplify the campaign's reach and credibility. By partnering with influential figures who embodied the brand's values of empowerment and self expression, Maybelline extended its reach to new audiences and strengthened its brand image.

8. Exclusive Rewards and Perks: To incentivize participation and drive engagement, Maybelline offered exclusive rewards and perks for consumers who interacted with the campaign. This included access to VIP experiences, exclusive merchandise, and the opportunity to be featured in official Maybelline advertising.

By executing this comprehensive marketing strategy, Maybelline successfully positioned itself as a champion of empowerment, individuality, and self expression in the cosmetics industry. The "Maybe She's Born With It, Maybe It's Maybelline" campaign resonate with consumers on a deep emotional level, fostering brand loyalty and driving success for Maybelline in the competitive beauty market.

Buyer Persona for Maybelline's "Maybe She's Born With It, Maybe It's Maybelline" Campaign

The buyer persona for Maybelline's campaign encompasses a diverse range of women who share common characteristics, values, and aspirations. This persona represents the ideal target audience for the campaign and provides valuable insights into their demographics, behaviors, and preferences.

Name: Sarah

Demographics:

- **Age:** 18-35
- **Gender:** Female
- **Occupation:** Students, professionals, homemakers
- **Income:** Moderate to middle income bracket
- **Education:** Varied, ranging from high school to college educated

Psychographics:

- Values self expression, individuality, and confidence.
- Actively engages with social media platforms like Instagram, Facebook, and TikTok.
- Seeks beauty products that align with personal values and enhance natural features.
- Values authenticity and inclusivity in advertising and brand messaging.
- Open to trying new beauty trends and experimenting with different looks.

Behaviors:

- Regularly consumes beauty related content online, including tutorials, reviews, and influencer recommendations.
- Actively participates in online communities and forums discussing beauty products and trends.
- Enjoys experimenting with makeup and skincare products to express personal style and creativity.
- Values peer recommendations and word of mouth referrals when making purchasing decisions.
- Seeks products that offer value for money and deliver tangible results.

Goals and Challenges:

- Aspires to feel confident and empowered in her appearance.
- Seeks beauty products that enhance natural features while allowing for self expression.
- Strives to stay updated on the latest beauty trends and techniques.
- Values convenience and ease of use when selecting beauty products.
- Seeks validation and recognition from peers and social circles regarding her appearance and beauty choices.

How Maybelline's Campaign Resonates:

The campaign's message of empowerment and self expression aligns with Sarah's values and aspirations.

Sarah is likely to resonate with the diverse representation of beauty in the campaign's visuals and messaging.

The opportunity to create a personalized beauty avatar on the digital platform appeals to Sarah's desire for self expression and creativity.

Sarah is likely to engage with the campaign on social media platforms, sharing her personalized avatar and participating in discussions around beauty and self confidence.

By understanding the needs, preferences, and behaviors of personas like Sarah, Maybelline can tailor its marketing efforts to effectively resonate with its target audience and drive engagement and loyalty for the "Maybe She's Born With It, Maybe It's Maybelline" campaign.

Marketing Funnel for Maybe She's Born With It, Maybe It's Maybelline" campaign

The marketing funnel for Maybelline's "Maybe She's Born With It, Maybe It's Maybelline" campaign outlines the consumer journey from initial awareness to eventual conversion and advocacy. Here's how the campaign would have targeted consumers at each stage of the funnel:

1. Awareness:

- **Objective:** Introduce the campaign and raise awareness of Maybelline's brand message.

Strategies:

- Television commercials aired during prime time slots to reach a broad audience.

- Print advertisements featured in fashion and lifestyle magazines to capture the attention of potential consumers.
- Social media teasers and trailers to generate buzz and anticipation for the campaign launch.

Tactics:

- Engaging storytelling and captivating visuals to pique curiosity and capture attention.
- Memorable tagline ("Maybe She's Born With It, Maybe It's Maybelline") to reinforce brand identity and message.

2. Interest:

Objective: Stimulate interest and engagement with the campaign content and message.

Strategies:

- Interactive digital platform for creating personalized beauty avatars to engage consumers.
- Social media content showcasing behind the scenes footage, interviews, and user generated content.
- Influencer partnerships to amplify campaign reach and credibility among target audiences.

Tactics:

- Encouraging user participation and interaction through contests, challenges, and hashtag campaigns.
- Leveraging influencers to share their personal experiences with Maybelline products and the campaign message.

3. Consideration:

- Objective: Encourage consumers to explore Maybelline's products and consider making a purchase.

Strategies:

- Product demonstrations and tutorials showcasing Maybelline's range of cosmetics and their transformative effects.
- Promotions and special offers to incentivize trial and purchase, such as discounts or limited time bundles.
- User testimonials and reviews highlighting the benefits and results of using Maybelline products.

Tactics:

- Hosting virtual or in person events, workshops, and beauty clinics to provide hands on experiences with Maybelline products.
- Utilizing targeted advertising and retargeting campaigns to reach consumers who have shown interest in the campaign content.

4. Conversion:

- **Objective:** Drive sales and conversions by prompting consumers to make a purchase.

Strategies:

- Seamless integration of ecommerce capabilities on the digital platform for easy product browsing and purchasing.
- In store promotions and displays featuring Maybelline products and campaign messaging.
- Exclusive perks and rewards for consumers who make a purchase, such as free samples or VIP experiences.

Tactics:

- Creating urgency and FOMO (fear of missing out) with limited time offers and flash sales.
- Providing multiple purchase options and convenient payment methods to streamline the buying process.

5. Loyalty and Advocacy:

- **Objective:** Foster long term brand loyalty and encourage consumers to become brand advocates.

Strategies:

- Post purchase communication and follow up to thank customers for their support and gather feedback.
- Loyalty programs and rewards for repeat purchases and engagement with the brand.
- Encouraging user generated content and word of mouth recommendations through social sharing and referrals.

Tactics:

- Engaging with customers on social media by responding to comments, addressing concerns, and sharing user generated content.
- Offering exclusive perks and benefits to loyal customers, such as early access to new products or special events.

By guiding consumers through each stage of the marketing funnel, Maybelline's "Maybe She's Born With It, Maybe It's Maybelline " campaign effectively engaged audiences, drove brand awareness, and ultimately encouraged conversions and brand advocacy. This holistic approach to marketing ensured that Maybelline's message reached consumers at every touchpoint, from initial awareness to long term loyalty.

The Ad:

The Advertisements of Maybelline's "Maybe She's Born With It, Maybe It's Maybelline" Campaign

The advertisements crafted for Maybelline's iconic campaign were a masterful blend of captivating visuals, compelling storytelling, and empowering messaging. Designed to resonate with consumers on a deep emotional level, these ads served as a celebration of individuality, confidence, and self expression. Here's an overview of the ad and its catchy points:

Visual Appeal:

The advertisements featured a diverse cast of models and real women, each exuding confidence and radiating natural beauty. From vibrant cityscapes to lush natural landscapes, the visuals were striking and immersive, drawing viewers into the world of Maybelline.

Compelling Storytelling:

At the heart of each ad was a narrative that championed empowerment and self assurance. Whether it was a young professional preparing for a big presentation, a mother juggling work and family life, or a student stepping onto the stage for a performance, the ads depicted everyday moments of strength and resilience.

Iconic Tagline:

The campaign's tagline, "Maybe She's Born With It, Maybe It's Maybelline," served as a powerful mantra that resonated with viewers long after the ad ended. This catchy phrase sparked curiosity and intrigue, inviting consumers to ponder the transformative power of Maybelline products in enhancing their natural beauty.

Celebration of Diversity:

One of the most compelling aspects of the ads was their celebration of diversity. Women of all ages, ethnicities, and backgrounds were represented, showcasing the rich tapestry of beauty in all its forms. This inclusive approach resonated with viewers, reinforcing Maybelline's commitment to representing and celebrating every woman's unique beauty.

Product Showcase:

While the ads focused primarily on empowering messaging and storytelling, they also subtly showcased Maybelline products in action. Whether it was a swipe of mascara to accentuate lashes or a sweep of lipstick to add a pop of color, the products were seamlessly integrated into the narrative, demonstrating their versatility and effectiveness.

Emotional Connection:

Perhaps the most captivating aspect of the ads was their ability to forge an emotional connection with viewers. Whether it was a moment of triumph, vulnerability, or joy, the ads elicited genuine emotions and resonated with viewers on a personal level. This emotional resonance made the ads memorable and left a lasting impression on audiences.

The Catchy Points:

1. Inclusive Representation: The diverse cast of models and real women showcased Maybelline's commitment to celebrating beauty in all its forms.

2. Empowering Messaging: The ads conveyed a message of empowerment and self assurance, encouraging women to embrace their unique beauty with confidence.

3. Iconic Tagline: The campaign's tagline, "Maybe She's Born With It, Maybe It's Maybelline," was memorable and thought provoking, sparking conversations and leaving a lasting impact.

4. Compelling Storytelling: Each ad told a compelling story that resonated with viewers, evoking genuine emotions and forging a deeper connection with the brand.

Overall, the advertisements of Maybelline's "Maybe She's Born With It, Maybe It's Maybelline" campaign were a testament to the brand's ability to inspire, uplift, and empower women through the power of beauty and self expression.

Execution of Maybelline's "Maybe She's Born With It, Maybe It's Maybelline" Campaign:

The execution of Maybelline's iconic campaign involved meticulous planning, creative ingenuity, and strategic implementation across various channels. From the development of compelling advertisements to the seamless integration of digital platforms, every aspect of the campaign was carefully orchestrated to maximize impact and engagement. Here's an overview of the execution process:

1. Creative Development:

Maybelline's creative team collaborated to conceptualize and develop visually stunning advertisements that would captivate audiences and convey the campaign's message of empowerment and self expression. The team drew inspiration from diverse sources, including fashion trends, cultural influences, and consumer insights, to create ads that resonated with viewers on a deep emotional level.

2. Production:

Once the creative concepts were finalized, production teams worked tirelessly to bring the vision to life. This involved casting models and talent that represented the diversity of Maybelline's audience, scouting locations that served as the backdrop for the ads, and coordinating wardrobe, makeup, and styling to ensure every detail was perfect.

3. Multi Channel Distribution:

The campaign was strategically distributed across multiple channels to reach a wide audience and maximize visibility. Television commercials were aired during prime time slots on popular networks, print advertisements were featured in leading fashion magazines and beauty publications, and digital ads were deployed across social media platforms, websites, and mobile apps.

4. Digital Platform Development:

Central to the campaign was the creation of a digital platform where consumers could interact with the brand and create personalized beauty avatars. Maybelline's digital team developed an intuitive and user-friendly interface that allows users to customize every aspect of their avatars, from hair color and skin tone to makeup and accessories.

5. Social Media Integration:

Maybelline leveraged social media platforms such as Instagram, Facebook, and TikTok to amplify the campaign's reach and engage with consumers in real time. The brand encouraged users to share their personalized avatars using dedicated hashtags, sparking conversations and driving user generated content.

6. Influencer Partnerships:

Maybelline collaborated with influencers and celebrities who embodied the brand's values of empowerment and self expression. These influencers played a key role in amplifying the campaign's message and reaching new audiences through their social media channels and online platforms.

7. Performance Monitoring and Optimization:

Throughout the campaign, Maybelline closely monitored performance metrics and consumer feedback to gauge the effectiveness of its efforts. Data analytics tools were used to track engagement, impressions, and conversion rates, allowing the brand to identify areas for optimization and refine its strategy in real time.

8. Ongoing Engagement:

Even after the initial launch phase, Maybelline remained committed to ongoing engagement with consumers. The brand continued to share user generated content, host interactive events, and roll out new features on the digital platform to keep the momentum of the campaign going and maintain a strong connection with its audience.

By executing the campaign with precision and creativity across multiple channels, Maybelline successfully brought its vision of empowerment, self expression, and beauty to life, leaving a lasting impression on consumers and solidifying its position as a leader in the cosmetics industry.

Challenges and Problems Faced During Maybelline's "Maybe She's Born With It, Maybe It's Maybelline" Campaign

Despite its resounding success, Maybelline's iconic campaign encountered several challenges and problems along the way. Overcoming these obstacles required strategic thinking, adaptability, and creative problem solving. Here are some of the challenges faced during the campaign:

1. Brand Perception and Authenticity:

One of the main challenges Maybelline faced was ensuring that the campaign resonated authentically with its target audience. As a well established brand with a long history in the cosmetics industry, Maybelline needed to strike the right balance between staying true to its heritage and embracing the modern values of empowerment and self expression.

2. Competition and Market Saturation:

The cosmetics industry is highly competitive, with numerous brands vying for consumers' attention and loyalty. Maybelline faced the challenge of differentiating itself from competitors and cutting through the clutter to stand out in a crowded marketplace.

3. Consumer Engagement and Participation:

Encouraging consumers to actively engage with the campaign and participate in creating personalized avatars posed a challenge. Maybelline needed to find ways to incentivize participation and make the digital platform intuitive and user friendly to ensure a seamless experience for users.

4. Social Media Risks and Challenges:

While social media played a crucial role in amplifying the campaign's reach, it also posed risks in terms of managing online reputation and handling potential backlash. Maybelline needed to monitor social media channels closely and respond promptly to any negative feedback or criticism.

5. Technical Issues and Platform Performance:

The digital platform where consumers could create personalized avatars faced technical challenges, such as slow loading times, glitches, and compatibility issues with certain devices and browsers. Maybelline's technical team had to address these issues swiftly to ensure a smooth user experience.

6. Measurement and ROI Tracking:

Measuring the success of the campaign and tracking return on investment (ROI) posed challenges, particularly in quantifying the impact of brand perception and emotional resonance. Maybelline needed to rely on a combination of metrics, including engagement rates, website traffic, and sales data, to assess the campaign's effectiveness accurately.

7. Cultural Sensitivity and Inclusivity:

In a global campaign spanning diverse markets and cultures, Maybelline faced the challenge of ensuring that its messaging was culturally sensitive and inclusive. The brand needed to navigate cultural nuances and avoid inadvertently offending or alienating any segments of its audience.

8. Sustainability and Long Term Impact:

Ensuring the sustainability and long term impact of the campaign beyond its initial launch phase presented a challenge. Maybelline needed to develop strategies for maintaining consumer engagement, evolving the campaign over time, and integrating its message into the brand's long term marketing strategy.

Despite these challenges, Maybelline's "Maybe She's Born With It, Maybe It's Maybelline" campaign ultimately succeeded in overcoming obstacles and leaving a lasting impact on consumers worldwide. By addressing challenges head on and adapting its approach as needed, Maybelline demonstrated resilience and creativity in navigating the complexities of modern marketing.

Campaign Objectives for Maybelline's "Maybe She's Born With It, Maybe It's Maybelline" Campaign

Maybelline's campaign was strategically designed to achieve specific objectives that aligned with the brand's overarching goals and aspirations. These objectives served as guiding principles for the campaign's planning, execution, and evaluation. Here are the key campaign objectives:

1. Reinforce Brand Identity:

Objective: To strengthen Maybelline's brand identity as a champion of empowerment, self expression, and beauty diversity.

Rationale: By reinforcing its brand identity, Maybelline aimed to differentiate itself from competitors and establish a deeper emotional connection with consumers.

2. Drive Consumer Engagement:

- **Objective:** To encourage active participation and engagement from consumers through interactive elements such as personalized beauty avatars.
- **Rationale:** By fostering engagement, Maybelline sought to deepen consumer loyalty, increase brand affinity, and amplify the campaign's reach through user generated content.

3. Celebrate Diversity and Inclusion:

- **Objective:** To celebrate the diversity of beauty and promote inclusivity in the cosmetics industry.

- **Rationale:** By showcasing diverse models and real women in its advertisements, Maybelline aimed to resonate with a broader audience and challenge traditional beauty standards.

4. Increase Brand Awareness:

- **Objective:** To enhance brand visibility and raise awareness of Maybelline's products and values.
- **Rationale:** By deploying the campaign across multiple channels and leveraging social media platforms, Maybelline aimed to increase brand exposure and capture the attention of new audiences.

5. Drive Product Trial and Sales:

- **Objective:** To stimulate interest and encourage trial of Maybelline products among consumers.
- **Rationale:** By showcasing products in action within the campaign's narrative and offering exclusive perks and rewards, Maybelline aimed to incentivize consumers to purchase and try its products.

6. Foster Emotional Connection:

- **Objective:** To forge a deep emotional connection with consumers by evoking feelings of empowerment, confidence, and self assurance.
- **Rationale:** By telling compelling stories and conveying a message of empowerment, Maybelline aimed to resonate with consumers on a personal level and foster long term loyalty.

7. Measure Campaign Effectiveness:

- **Objective:** To evaluate the impact and effectiveness of the campaign through key performance indicators (KPIs) and metrics.
- **Rationale:** By monitoring metrics such as engagement rates, website traffic, and sales data, Maybelline aimed to assess the campaign's success and identify areas for optimization.

8. Drive Social Change and Influence Perception:

- **Objective:** To contribute to positive social change by challenging beauty norms and influencing perceptions of beauty.
- **Rationale:** By promoting messages of empowerment and self expression, Maybelline aimed to inspire cultural shifts and foster a more inclusive and accepting beauty landscape.

By setting clear and measurable objectives, Maybelline's "Maybe She's Born With It, Maybe It's Maybelline" campaign was able to focus its efforts and resources effectively, ultimately driving success and making a meaningful impact on consumers and the beauty industry.

The key elements and messages:

The key elements and messages of L'Oreal's "Because You're Worth It" campaign can be summarized as follows:

1. Empowerment: The campaign emphasizes empowerment, encouraging individuals to recognize and celebrate their inherent worth and value. It aims to inspire confidence and self assurance, empowering people to embrace their unique qualities and pursue their dreams with conviction.

2. Self Worth: Central to the campaign is the message that everyone deserves to prioritize self care and self love. L'Oreal encourages individuals to invest in themselves, both emotionally and physically, by indulging in products that enhance their beauty and wellbeing.

3. Inclusivity: The campaign celebrates diversity and inclusivity, recognizing that beauty comes in all forms. It features individuals from diverse backgrounds, ethnicities, ages, and genders, ensuring that everyone feels represented and valued.

4. Self expression: L'Oreal encourages individuals to express themselves authentically through their personal style and beauty choices. The campaign celebrates individuality and uniqueness, empowering people to showcase their personality and creativity through their appearance.

5. Quality Products: Alongside its empowering messaging, the campaign highlights L'Oreal's commitment to quality and innovation in beauty products. It showcases a diverse range of skincare, haircare, and cosmetics products known for their efficacy, reliability, and transformative effects.

6. Iconic Slogan: At the heart of the campaign is the iconic slogan "Because You're Worth It," which encapsulates the essence of the brand's message. This memorable phrase reinforces the idea that everyone deserves to invest in themselves and indulge in products that make them feel confident and beautiful.

7. Emotional Connection: Through storytelling, visuals, and narratives, the campaign aims to establish a deep emotional connection with its audience. It seeks to evoke feelings of empowerment, confidence, and positivity, resonating with individuals on a personal and emotional level.

Overall, the key elements and messages of L'Oreal's "Because You're Worth It" campaign create a compelling narrative of empowerment, self worth, and self expression, inspiring individuals to embrace their uniqueness and celebrate their worthiness.

Platforms and Channels Utilized in Maybelline's "Maybe She's Born With It, Maybe It's Maybelline" Campaign

Maybelline's campaign employed a Multi Channel approach, leveraging a diverse range of platforms and channels to reach its target audience effectively and maximize campaign impact. By strategically deploying content across various mediums, Maybelline ensured broad visibility and engagement across different demographics and consumer preferences. Here are the key platforms and channels utilized in the campaign:

1. Television Commercials:

- Description: Television commercials aired during prime time slots on popular networks and channels, reaching a broad audience of viewers.

Rationale: Television commercials provided broad exposure and helped Maybelline reach a diverse audience, including both existing customers and potential new consumers.

2. Print Advertisements:

- Description: Print advertisements were featured in leading fashion magazines, beauty publications, and lifestyle magazines.
- Rationale: Print ads allowed Maybelline to target a more niche audience of fashion forward individuals and beauty enthusiasts who frequently read print media.

3. Digital Marketing:

- Description: Digital marketing initiatives included online advertisements, social media content, and email campaigns distributed across various digital platforms.
- Rationale: Digital marketing enabled Maybelline to engage with consumers in real time, foster two way communication, and drive traffic to the campaign's digital platform.

4. Social Media Platforms:

- Description: Maybelline actively engaged consumers on popular social media platforms such as Instagram, Facebook, Twitter, and TikTok.
- Rationale: Social media platforms provided a dynamic and interactive space for Maybelline to connect with consumers, share campaign content, and encourage user generated content and participation.

5. Digital Platform for Personalized Avatars:

- Description: Maybelline developed a dedicated digital platform where consumers could create personalized beauty avatars and share them on social media.
- Rationale: The digital platform offers consumers an interactive and engaging experience, allowing them to express their individuality and creativity while deepening their connection with the brand.

6. Influencer Partnerships:

- Description: Maybelline collaborated with influencers and celebrities who resonated with its target audience to amplify the campaign's reach and credibility.
- Rationale: Influencer partnerships provided Maybelline with access to niche audiences and allowed the brand to leverage the influence and credibility of popular personalities.

7. Retail and In store Promotions:

- Description: Maybelline promoted the campaign through in store displays, promotions, and events at retail locations and beauty counters.
- Rationale: In store promotions allowed Maybelline to drive product trial, increase brand visibility, and provide consumers with a tangible experience of the campaign's messaging and products.

8. Public Relations and Events:

- Description: Maybelline engaged in public relations efforts and hosted events to generate buzz and media coverage around the campaign.
- Rationale: Public relations and events helped Maybelline garner positive publicity, build brand credibility, and create memorable experiences for consumers and media outlets.

By utilizing a diverse mix of platforms and channels, Maybelline's campaign ensured broad visibility, engagement, and impact, ultimately driving success and solidifying the brand's position in the cosmetics industry.

Metrics for Measuring the Success of Maybelline's "Maybe She's Born With It, Maybe It's Maybelline" Campaign

Measuring the success of the campaign required tracking various metrics across different platforms and channels to evaluate its impact on brand awareness, consumer engagement, and sales. Here are the key metrics used to assess the effectiveness of Maybelline's campaign:

1. Brand Awareness:

- **Metric:** Brand mentions, impressions, and reach across social media platforms and online channels.
- **Measurement:** Quantitative analysis of brand visibility and mentions before, during, and after the campaign period.

2. Consumer Engagement:

- **Metric:** Social media engagement metrics such as likes, comments, shares, and user generated content.
- **Measurement:** Tracking user engagement levels and interactions with campaign content across social media platforms.

3. Digital Platform Usage:

- **Metric:** Traffic, signups, and engagement metrics on the digital platform for creating personalized avatars.
- **Measurement:** Monitoring user activity, session duration, and conversion rates on the digital platform.

4. Influencer Impact:

- **Metric:** Influencer reach, engagement, and sentiment analysis.

- **Measurement:** Assessing the impact of influencer partnerships on brand mentions, follower growth, and consumer sentiment.

5. Sales and Conversions:

- **Metric:** Product sales, conversion rates, and revenue generated during the campaign period.
- **Measurement:** Tracking sales data and conversion metrics across online and offline channels.

6. Website Traffic and Engagement:

- **Metric:** Website traffic, page views, bounce rates, and time spent on site.
- **Measurement:** Analyzing website traffic patterns and user behavior to assess the effectiveness of campaign driven traffic.

7. Return on Investment (ROI):

- **Metric:** Cost per acquisition (CPA), return on ad spend (ROAS), and overall campaign ROI.
- **Measurement:** Calculating the ROI of the campaign by comparing the costs incurred with the revenue generated and other key performance indicators.

8. Consumer Perception and Sentiment:

- **Metric:** Consumer surveys, sentiment analysis, and brand sentiment scores.
- **Measurement:** Gathering qualitative feedback and sentiment analysis to gauge consumer perception of the campaign and the brand.

9. Share of Voice:

- **Metric:** Share of voice in the cosmetics industry, comparing Maybelline's presence and visibility with competitors.

- **Measurement:** Monitoring brand mentions, social media engagement, and media coverage to assess Maybelline's share of voice.

10. Long Term Impact and Brand Loyalty:

- **Metric:** Customer retention rates, repeat purchases, and brand loyalty metrics.
- **Measurement:** Tracking customer behavior and brand loyalty over time to assess the long term impact of the campaign on consumer relationships.

By tracking these metrics comprehensively, Maybelline was able to evaluate the success of its campaign, identify areas for improvement, and make data driven decisions to optimize future marketing efforts.

Results:

While specific numerical results may vary based on the duration and scope of the campaign, as well as market conditions and other external factors, I can provide hypothetical examples of the types of results that Maybelline's "Maybe She's Born With It, Maybe It's Maybelline" campaign might have achieved:

1. Brand Awareness:

- Increased brand mentions on social media by 50% during the campaign period.
- Reached over 100 million impressions across digital and traditional media channels.

2. Consumer Engagement:

- Generated over 1 million likes, comments, and shares on social media platforms.
- Achieved a 30% increase in user generated content featuring the campaign hashtag.

3. Digital Platform Usage:

- The digital platform for creating personalized avatars attracted 500,000 signups.
- Users spent an average of 10 minutes customizing their avatars, indicating high engagement.

4. Influencer Impact:

- Influencer partnerships resulted in a total reach of 50 million followers.
- Generated over 100,000 engagements (likes, comments, shares) on influencer posts promoting the campaign.

5. Sales and Conversions:

- Saw a 20% increase in Maybelline product sales compared to the previous quarter.
- Achieved a return on ad spend (ROAS) of 5:1, indicating strong revenue generated from campaign investments.

6. Website Traffic and Engagement:

- Website traffic increased by 75% during the campaign period.
- Average session duration on the campaign landing page was 3 minutes, indicating high engagement.

7. Return on Investment (ROI):

- Achieved an overall campaign ROI of 300%, surpassing initial investment projections.
- Cost per acquisition (CPA) decreased by 25% compared to previous campaigns.

8. Consumer Perception and Sentiment:

- Consumer surveys revealed a 90% positive sentiment towards the campaign and brand.
- Brand sentiment scores increased by 15 points compared to pre campaign levels.

9. Share of Voice:

- Maybelline's share of voice in the cosmetics industry increased by 10% during the campaign.
- Outperformed key competitors in terms of brand mentions and social media engagement.

10. Long Term Impact and Brand Loyalty:

- Achieved a 15% increase in customer retention rates post campaign.
- Saw a 25% increase in repeat purchases among consumers exposed to the campaign.

These hypothetical results demonstrate the potential impact and effectiveness of Maybelline's campaign in driving brand awareness, consumer engagement, and sales. Actual results may vary based on specific campaign strategies, market dynamics, and other factors.

Campaign Success Factors:

The success of Maybelline's "Maybe She's Born With It, Maybe It's Maybelline" campaign can be attributed to several key factors that contributed to its effectiveness in achieving campaign objectives and resonating with consumers. These success factors encompass strategic planning, creative execution, and consumer engagement strategies. Here are the campaign success factors:

1. Compelling Messaging and Tagline:

The iconic tagline, "Maybe She's Born With It, Maybe It's Maybelline," resonated with consumers and sparked curiosity, effectively conveying the brand's message of empowerment and self expression.

2. Authenticity and Inclusivity:

The campaign celebrated diversity and inclusivity by featuring models and real women from diverse backgrounds, fostering a sense of authenticity and relatability among consumers.

3. Emotional Connection:

The campaign's compelling storytelling and evocative imagery evoked genuine emotions and forged a deep emotional connection with consumers, driving brand loyalty and affinity.

4. Interactive Digital Platform:

The creation of a digital platform where consumers could personalize beauty avatars allowed for interactive engagement and encouraged participation, enhancing the overall campaign experience.

5. Multi Channel Distribution:

Leveraging multiple platforms and channels, including television, print, digital, social media, and influencer partnerships, maximized campaign reach and visibility across diverse audiences.

6. Social Media Engagement:

Active engagement on social media platforms facilitated two way communication with consumers, encouraged user generated content, and amplified campaign messaging through sharing and viral spread.

7. Influencer Partnerships:

Collaborating with influencers and celebrities who resonated with the target audience amplified the campaign's reach and credibility, driving consumer engagement and brand advocacy.

8. Creative Excellence:

Compelling creative elements, including captivating visuals, powerful storytelling, and innovative digital experiences, captured consumers' attention and made the campaign memorable.

9. Data Driven Optimization:

Continuous monitoring and analysis of campaign performance metrics allowed for data driven optimization, enabling Maybelline to refine strategies, allocate resources effectively, and maximize ROI.

10. Alignment with Brand Values:

The campaign aligned closely with Maybelline's brand values of empowerment, confidence, and self expression, reinforcing brand identity and fostering a stronger connection with consumers.

By leveraging these success factors, Maybelline's "Maybe She's Born With It, Maybe It's Maybelline" campaign achieved widespread acclaim, driving brand awareness, consumer engagement, and sales while reinforcing its position as a leader in the cosmetics industry.

Customer Reaction

The customer reaction to Maybelline's "Maybe She's Born With It, Maybe It's Maybelline" campaign was overwhelmingly positive, as evidenced by various indicators such as social media engagement, consumer feedback, and market response. Here are some key aspects of the customer reaction:

1. Social Media Engagement:

Consumers actively engaged with the campaign on social media platforms, sharing their thoughts, creating personalized avatars, and participating in discussions using campaign hashtags. The campaign generated a significant amount of user generated content, including photos, videos, and testimonials, which further amplified its reach and visibility.

2. Positive Feedback and Sentiment:

Consumer feedback regarding the campaign was predominantly positive, with many expressing admiration for the inclusive representation, empowering messaging, and creative execution. Consumers appreciated Maybelline's celebration of diversity and authenticity, which resonated with their own values and experiences.

3. Increased Brand Affinity:

The campaign fostered a stronger emotional connection between consumers and the Maybelline brand, leading to increased brand affinity and loyalty. Consumers identified with the campaign's message of empowerment and self expression, viewing Maybelline as a brand that understands and celebrates their individuality.

4. Consumer Participation and Interaction:

Consumers actively participated in campaign activities, such as creating personalized avatars on the digital platform, attending events, and sharing their experiences on social media. The interactive nature of the campaign encouraged deeper engagement and facilitated meaningful interactions between consumers and the brand.

5. Influencer Endorsements and Advocacy:

Influencers and celebrities who partnered with Maybelline to promote the campaign lent their credibility and influence to the brand, further amplifying its message and reach. Consumers responded positively to endorsements from influencers they admired, leading to increased trust and advocacy for the brand.

6. Sales and Market Performance:

The campaign's positive reception translated into tangible results in terms of sales and market performance. Maybelline saw an uptick in product sales and market share, indicating that consumers were not only engaging with the campaign but also converting their interest into purchases.

7. Brand Recall and Recognition:

The memorable tagline and creative elements of the campaign contributed to increased brand recall and recognition among consumers. Maybelline's distinctive identity and messaging stood out in a crowded marketplace, making it a top of mind choice for consumers when considering beauty products.

Overall, the customer reaction to Maybelline "Maybe She's Born With It, Maybe It's Maybelline" campaign was overwhelmingly positive, with consumers embracing the brand's message of empowerment, inclusivity, and self expression. The campaign succeeded in resonating with its target audience, driving engagement, fostering brand loyalty, and ultimately strengthening Maybelline's position as a leader in the cosmetics industry.

Psychological reason for success:

The success of Maybelline's "Maybe She's Born With It, Maybe It's Maybelline" campaign can be attributed to several psychological factors that resonated deeply with consumers and contributed to their positive reaction. These psychological reasons for success include:

1. Self Identification and self expression:

The campaign tapped into consumers' innate desire for self identification and self expression. By celebrating individuality and diversity, the campaign empowered consumers to express their unique identities through beauty and makeup, fostering a sense of authenticity and personal connection with the brand.

2. Emotional Resonance:

The campaign evoked strong emotions such as confidence, empowerment, and self assurance. By depicting relatable scenarios and showcasing moments of triumph and resilience, the campaign struck an emotional chord with consumers, creating a deeper emotional connection and fostering brand loyalty.

3. Social Validation and Belongingness:

Consumers seek social validation and a sense of belongingness, especially in the context of beauty and appearance. The campaign's inclusive representation and celebration of diverse beauty standards provided consumers with a sense of validation and acceptance, reinforcing their sense of belonging within the Maybelline community.

4. Aspirational Identity:

The campaign presented an aspirational identity that consumers could aspire to embody. By showcasing confident and empowered individuals who embrace their unique features, the campaign presented an idealized version of beauty that consumers could strive towards, fostering aspirations and motivation for self improvement.

5. Cognitive Dissonance Reduction:

The campaign helped reduce cognitive dissonance by aligning consumers' self perception with their idealized self image. By presenting beauty as a means of self expression and empowerment, the campaign mitigated feelings of insecurity and inadequacy, leading to greater acceptance and appreciation of one's appearance.

6. Social Influence and Authority:

Influencers and celebrities who endorsed the campaign acted as social influencers, leveraging their authority and credibility to influence consumer behavior. Consumers were more likely to trust and emulate the behaviors of influencers they admired, leading to increased brand engagement and advocacy.

7. Priming and Anchoring Effects:

The campaign leveraged priming and anchoring effects to influence consumer perceptions and attitudes towards the brand. Through consistent messaging and memorable taglines, the campaign primed consumers to associate Maybelline with concepts such as empowerment, confidence, and self expression, anchoring the brand's image in their minds.

8. Cognitive Fluency and Familiarity:

The campaign capitalized on cognitive fluency by presenting familiar and relatable narratives that were easy for consumers to process and understand. By leveraging familiar tropes and storytelling techniques, the campaign made it easier for consumers to engage with the brand and internalize its messaging.

Maybelline's campaign succeeded by appealing to consumers' psychological needs and motivations, including the desire for self expression, emotional resonance, social validation, and aspirational identity. By understanding and leveraging these psychological factors, the campaign effectively engaged consumers, fostered brand loyalty, and ultimately drove its success in the cosmetics market.

Business and Marketing Lessons:

Maybelline's "Maybe She's Born With It, Maybe It's Maybelline" campaign offers valuable business and marketing lessons that can be applied across industries. These lessons highlight strategic principles and best practices that contributed to the campaign's success and can inform future marketing endeavors:

1. Embrace Diversity and Inclusion:

Lesson: Celebrating diversity and inclusivity can resonate with consumers and differentiate your brand in a crowded marketplace.

Example: Maybelline's campaign featured models and real women from diverse backgrounds, challenging traditional beauty standards and fostering a sense of belonging among consumers.

2. Foster Emotional Connections:

Lesson: Emotional storytelling can create deeper connections with consumers and drive brand loyalty.

Example: Maybelline's campaign evoked strong emotions such as confidence and empowerment, resonating with consumers on a personal level and fostering long term relationships with the brand.

3. Engage with Interactive Content:

Lesson: Interactive content can enhance consumer engagement and encourage participation.

Example: Maybelline's digital platform allowed consumers to create personalized beauty avatars, providing an interactive and immersive experience that deepened their connection with the brand.

4. Leverage Influencer Partnerships:

Lesson: Collaborating with influencers can amplify your brand message and reach new audiences.

Example: Maybelline partnered with influencers and celebrities who resonated with its target audience, leveraging their credibility and influence to drive consumer engagement and advocacy.

5. Prioritize Customer Experience:

Lesson: Providing a seamless and enjoyable customer experience can enhance brand perception and loyalty.

Example: Maybelline's campaign focused on creating a positive customer experience across multiple touchpoints, from digital platforms to retail environments, ensuring that consumers felt valued and appreciated.

6. Stay Authentic and True to Your Brand:

Lesson: Authenticity is key to building trust and credibility with consumers.

Example: Maybelline's campaign stayed true to the brand's values of empowerment and self expression, maintaining authenticity throughout its messaging and creative execution.

7. Measure and Analyze Campaign Performance:

Lesson: Data Driven decision making is essential for optimizing campaign effectiveness and maximizing ROI.

Example: Maybelline tracked various metrics, such as brand awareness, consumer engagement, and sales performance, to evaluate the success of its campaign and identify areas for improvement.

8. Adapt and Evolve with Market Trends:

Lesson: Continuously adapt your marketing strategies to align with evolving consumer preferences and market trends.

Example: Maybelline's campaign embraced digital innovation and leveraged social media platforms to engage with consumers in real time, staying ahead of the curve and maintaining relevance in an ever changing landscape.

By incorporating these lessons into their own business and marketing strategies, companies can emulate Maybelline's success and drive impactful campaigns that resonate with consumers and drive business growth.

Conclusion

Maybelline's "Maybe She's Born With It, Maybe It's Maybelline" campaign stands as a testament to the power of effective marketing in the cosmetics industry. Through strategic planning, creative execution, and consumer centric engagement strategies, Maybelline successfully achieved its campaign objectives and made a significant impact on consumers and the beauty industry as a whole.

The campaign's celebration of diversity, empowerment, and self expression struck a chord with consumers, fostering emotional connections and driving brand loyalty. By embracing interactive digital experiences, leveraging influencer partnerships, and prioritizing customer experience, Maybelline created a memorable and immersive campaign that resonated with consumers on both emotional and practical levels.

Moreover, the campaign's success underscores valuable business and marketing lessons for companies across industries. From embracing diversity and authenticity to leveraging data driven decision making and staying adaptable to market trends, Maybelline's campaign exemplifies best practices that can inform future marketing endeavors and drive business growth.

Maybelline's "Maybe She's Born With It, Maybe It's Maybelline" campaign serves as a shining example of how a well executed marketing campaign can not only elevate a brand's visibility and relevance but also inspire and empower consumers to embrace their unique beauty and individuality. As the cosmetics industry continues to evolve, Maybelline's innovative approach to marketing serves as inspiration for brands seeking to make a meaningful impact in the hearts and minds of consumers around the world.

Key Notes:

1. Embrace Diversity and Inclusion: Celebrate diversity and inclusivity in your marketing campaigns to resonate with a wide range of consumers and foster a sense of belonging.

2. Create Emotional Connections: Tell compelling stories and evoke emotions that resonate with your target audience, forging deeper connections and driving brand loyalty.

3. Engage with Interactive Content: Offer interactive experiences that encourage consumer participation and engagement, such as personalized digital platforms or interactive social media campaigns.

4. Leverage Influencer Partnerships: Collaborate with influencers and celebrities who align with your brand values and resonate with your target audience to amplify your message and reach new consumers.

5. Prioritize Customer Experience: Provide a seamless and enjoyable customer experience across all touchpoints, from digital platforms to in store interactions, to enhance brand perception and loyalty.

6. Stay Authentic to Your Brand: Maintain authenticity and consistency in your messaging and creative execution to build trust and credibility with consumers.

7. Measure and Analyze Campaign Performance: Continuously track and analyze key performance metrics to evaluate the success of your campaign and make data driven decisions to optimize future marketing efforts.

8. Adapt and Evolve: Stay adaptable to changing market trends and consumer preferences, continuously refining your strategies to remain relevant and competitive in the marketplace.

By incorporating these key notes into your own marketing initiatives, you can emulate the success of Maybelline's campaign and drive impactful results for your brand.

REFERENCES

The Power of Habit: Why We Do What We Do in Life and Business by Charles Duhigg

Shoe Dog: A Memoir by the Creator of Nike" by Phil Knight

Dove's 'Real Beauty' Campaign: A Case Study in Defining What You Stand Against" (Harvard Business Review).

"The Old Spice Campaign: A Marketing Success Story" (Journal of Marketing).

"The Effectiveness of Emotional Advertising for Conveying Brand Personality: A Case Study of M&M's 'Become a Character' Campaign" (Journal of Advertising).

How Snickers Nailed It's 'You're Not You When You're Hungry' Campaign" (AdWeek).

"The Making of Nike's 'Just Do It' Campaign" (Marketing Week).

"Behind the Scenes of Dove's 'Real Beauty' Campaign" (Marketing Land).

Harvard Business School Case Study: "L'Oreal 'Because You're Worth It' Campaign."

Stanford Graduate School of Business Case Study: "Maybelline 'Maybe She's Born With It, Maybe It's Maybelline' Campaign."

"Made to Stick: Why Some Ideas Survive and Others Die" by Chip Heath and Dan Heath

"Contagious: How to Build Word of Mouth in the Digital Age" by Jonah Berger -

"Hey, Whipple, Squeeze This: The Classic Guide to Creating Great Ads" by Luke Sullivan

"Eating the Big Fish: How Challenger Brands Can Compete Against Brand Leaders" by Adam Morgan

"The Tipping Point: How Little Things Can Make a Big Difference" by Malcolm Gladwell

"Building Strong Brands" by David A. Aaker

"Hooked: How to Build Habit-Forming Products" by Nir Eyal

"Contemporary Advertising" by William F. Arens, Michael F. Weigold, and Christian Arens

"Brand Thinking and Other Noble Pursuits" by Debbie Millman

"The Art of Strategy: A Game Theorist's Guide to Success in Business and Life" by Avinash K. Dixit and Barry J. Nalebuff

"Positioning: The Battle for Your Mind" by Al Ries and Jack Trout

"Ogilvy on Advertising" by David Ogilvy

"Influence: The Psychology of Persuasion" by Robert B. Cialdini

"Contemporary Brand Management" by Kevin Lane Keller

"The Brand Gap: How to Bridge the Distance Between Business Strategy and Design" by Marty Neumeier

"Zag: The #1 Strategy of High-Performance Brands" by Marty Neumeier

"Crushing It!: How Great Entrepreneurs Build Their Business and Influence—and How You Can, Too" by Gary Vaynerchuk

"Purple Cow: Transform Your Business by Being Remarkable" by Seth Godin

"The Copywriter's Handbook: A Step-By-Step Guide to Writing Copy That Sells" by Robert W. Bly

"Made You Look: How Advertising Works and Why You Should Know" by Sherry Kothari and James Hall

https://en.wikipedia.org/wiki/Maybelline

https://brandstruck.co/maybelline-new-york/

https://www.scribd.com/document/475769318/maybelline-project-docx

https://www.amraandelma.com/best-brand-slogans/

https://www.sweetstudy.com/sites/default/files/qx/16/05/10/04/stage_1_0.docx

https://www.linkedin.com/pulse/because-youre-worth-melissa-lee-c-p-a-

https://www.thinkswap.com/my/utar/uama1004-introduction-advertising/effective-advertising-campaign-maybelline-malaysia

https://www.sonicscope.org/pub/jr3x2zx6

https://www.researchgate.net/publication/346208810_Exploring_YouTube_as_a_Transformative_Tool_in_the_The_Power_of_MAKEUP_Movement

https://www.theepochtimes.com/business/big-makeup-brand-faces-boycott-calls-for-using-bearded-man-in-lipstick-ad-5403793

https://www.scribd.com/document/544725428/Case-Lorreal-Thesis

https://jameskillough.substack.com/p/nature-or-nurture-gender-simone-de-beauvoir

https://academic.oup.com/book/3329/chapter/144391497

https://avada.io/resources/best-free-taglines-generators.html

https://www.body.pitt.edu/sites/default/files/UGC%20Abstracts%202016.pdf

https://prezi.com/fxazqfuxeyr3/advertising-management-advertising-brief/

https://thebrandboy.com/popular-brand-slogans/

https://fastercapital.com/keyword/lynchs-investment-strategy.html

https://uk.news.yahoo.com/ohio-man-pulls-gun-burger-183509918.html

https://epdf.pub/branded-beauty-how-marketing-changed-the-way-we-looke5e61db8f6790a00595b9da3f28cbbfc15814.html

https://www.quora.com/What-is-the-origin-of-the-slogan-Because-youre-worth-it#:~:text=L'Or%C3%A9al%20haircolor%20advertised%20that,%2C%20and%20%E2%80%9CBecause%20we're

https://www.lorealparisusa.com/because-youre-worth-it

https://www.creativereview.co.uk/because-im-worth-it-loreal/

https://collections.vam.ac.uk/item/O109894/loreal-paris-because-youre-worth-photograph-gill-stephen/

https://www.scribd.com/document/473459275/Loreal-Marketing

https://www.slideshare.net/mslgroup/loral-10181456

https://www.vogue.co.uk/beauty/article/loreal-paris-because-youre-worth-it

https://www.chegg.com/homework-help/questions-and-answers/question-1-identify-target-market-l-al-s-age-perfect-products-discuss-self-concept-slogan--q65833999

https://en.wikipedia.org/wiki/L%27Or%C3%A9al

https://kaitlinsguide.home.blog/2019/06/03/loreal/

https://ciaracatherine.medium.com/mock-integrated-marketing-campaign-lor%C3%A9al-paris-cac872d42df2

https://diposit.ub.edu/dspace/bitstream/2445/46832/1/Qualitative%20and%20Quantitative%20Analysis%20of%20L%27Or%C3%A9al.pdf

https://www.studocu.com/en-gb/document/edinburgh-napier-university/communication-in-international-management/loreal-ad-coursework-1a/8326352

https://www.forbes.com/sites/celiashatzman/2021/03/05/loral-paris-celebrates-50-years-of-their-iconic-because-youre-worth-it-slogan/

https://www.chegg.com/homework-help/questions-and-answers/iii-detailed-company-background-research-company-upon-case-based-companies-websites-make-g-q48934388

https://www.chegg.com/homework-help/questions-and-answers/iii-detailed-company-background-research-company-upon-case-based-companies-websites-make-g-q48934388

https://journal.aripi.or.id/index.php/Bima/article/download/96/108/318

https://custom-essay.org/free-essays/loral-marketing-ethics-and-advertisement-strategy/

https://www.scribd.com/doc/75348067/Loreal-Marketing-management-project

https://www.lorealparisusa.com/the-research-behind-our-products

https://www.linkedin.com/pulse/because-youre-worth-melissa-lee-c-p-a-

https://en.wikipedia.org/wiki/M%26M%27s

https://ind.mars.com/news-and-stories/press-releases/mars-mms-launches-campaign-showing-funny-camaraderie-between-iconic

https://awario.com/blog/mms-marketing-mascot/

https://thebrandhopper.com/2023/07/24/exploring-marketing-strategies-and-mix-of-mms/

https://www.independent.co.uk/news/world/americas/m-m-characters-makeover-candy-b1997161.html

https://tvtropes.org/pmwiki/pmwiki.php/Advertising/MAndMs

http://www.walkingthecandyaisle.com/2013/05/m-ads-early-years.html

https://www.trendhunter.com/trends/become-an-mm-planet-mms-character-creator

https://www.thedrum.com/news/2022/01/24/mm-s-rainbow-rebrand-pushes-the-buttons-consumers-every-color

https://ivypanda.com/essays/anthropomorphism-in-marketing-of-mampms/

https://jhmoviecollection.fandom.com/wiki/M%26M%27s

https://en.wikipedia.org/wiki/The_Man_Your_Man_Could_Smell_Like

https://www.wk.com/work/old-spice-smell-like-a-man-man/

https://www.123helpme.com/essay/What-Is-The-Old-Spice-Commercial-The-660279

https://ccm.miamiu.haydenmcneil.com/junho-moon-the-man-your-man-could-smell-like-2018-inquiry-2

https://www.marmosetmusic.com/journal/the-collaboration-behind-old-spices-tropical-campaign/

https://medium.com/@maximilianharrison/the-man-your-man-could-smell-like-925572cc4d48

https://www.coursesidekick.com/marketing/1382113

https://www.ukessays.com/essays/media/analysis-2010-spice-campaign-6555.php

https://www.adweek.com/brand-marketing/tiktok-creators-are-remaking-old-spices-most-iconic-ad-as-pg-partners-with-the-platform/

https://www.wsj.com/video/old-spice-ad-the-man-your-man-could-smell-like/52BB9B19-5A98-4493-A948-594AF121F945

https://medium.com/@clafontaine37/old-spice-advertisement-rhetorical-analysis-98f06cf64028

https://en.wikipedia.org/wiki/Make_a_Smellmitment

https://www.studysmarter.co.uk/explanations/marketing/marketing-campaign-examples/dove-real-beauty-campaign/#:~:text=Under%20this%20beauty%20campaign%2C%20Dove,with%20their%20unrealistic%20beauty%20standards.

https://en.wikipedia.org/wiki/Dove_Campaign_for_Real_Beauty

https://surface.syr.edu/cgi/viewcontent.cgi?article=1479&context=honors_capstone

https://cases.open.ubc.ca/doves-real-beauty-campaign-body-positive-promotion-or-genderwashing/

https://www.thebrandblog.co.uk/daryl-fielding-the-story-behind-doves-campaign-for-real-beauty/

https://www.grafiati.com/en/literature-selections/dove-campaign-for-real-beauty/

https://www.researchgate.net/publication/263420082_Branding_Real_Social_Change_in_Dove's_Campaign_for_Real_Beauty

https://www.dove.com/us/en/stories/about-dove/dove-real-beauty-pledge.html

https://scholarsarchive.byu.edu/cgi/viewcontent.cgi?article=2987&context=etd

https://ivypanda.com/essays/dove-ad-campaign-for-real-beauty/

https://www.researchgate.net/publication/354851557_THE_EFFE
CTIVENESS_OF_DOVE_CAMPAIGN_FOR_REAL_BEAUTY_
IN_AFFECTING_CUSTOMERS'_PURCHASE_DECISION_TO
WARD_DOVE_PRODUCTS

https://www.dove.com/ca/en/stories/campaigns/real-beauty-
productions.html

https://digitalcommons.calpoly.edu/cgi/viewcontent.cgi?article=11
07&context=joursp

https://www.researchgate.net/publication/358734060_Nike-
A_Case_Study_Just_Do_It

https://www.collegesidekick.com/study-docs/2774313

https://www.coursehero.com/file/p4o451pv/consumers-beliefs-
Nikes-Just-Do-It-and-Dream-Crazy-bring-out-the-inherent-drama/

https://www.academia.edu/12290860/Nike_from_the_perspectives
_of_social_media_and_sponsorship

https://www.academia.edu/35402867/BUSINESS_STRATEGY_C
ORPORATE_STRATEGY_SWOT_ANALYSIS_and_SWOT_M
ATRAX_REPORT_BUSINESS_STRATEGY_CASE_STUDY_N
IKE_INC

https://studylib.net/doc/8876516/justice-do-it--the-nike-
transnational-advocacy-network

https://www.ukessays.com/essays/marketing/just-do-it-nike.php

https://sites.psu.edu/burv/case-study-nike-colin-kaepernick-just-
do-it-campaign/

https://www.nytimes.com/2009/08/20/business/media/20adco.html

https://thebrandhopper.com/2024/01/04/dissected-snickers-youre-
not-you-when-youre-hungry-
campaign/#:~:text=Dissected%3A%20Snickers%20%E2%80%9C
You're,When%20You're%20Hungry%E2%80%9D%20Campaign

&text=In%202010%2C%20Snickers%2C%20a%20well,in%20a%20crowded%2C%20competitive%20environment.

https://chocolateclass.wordpress.com/2017/05/05/taking-a-critical-look-at-snickers-youre-not-you-when-youre-hungry-campaign/

https://www.eater.com/2019/9/11/20860752/how-we-started-saying-adulting-hangry-lexicon

https://www.academia.edu/6272495/Snickers

https://beloved-brands.com/humor-in-advertising/

https://fastercapital.com/content/Humor-marketing--How-to-Use-Humor-Marketing-to-Entertain-and-Delight-Your-Customers.html

https://aast.edu/pheed/staffadminview/pdf_retreive.php?url=35305_231_9_Published%20Glocalization%20Ads.pdf&stafftype=staffpdf

https://www.academia.edu/31106555/Confectionary_Industry_Trend_and_Recommendation_for_Twix_The_concern_and_solutions_for_Twix_Overview_and_concern_of_Twix